AN ANTHOLOGY OF
NEW ZEALAND VERSE

AN ANTHOLOGY OF
NEW ZEALAND
VERSE

Selected by
ROBERT CHAPMAN
and
JONATHAN BENNETT

Geoffrey Cumberlege
OXFORD UNIVERSITY PRESS
London and Wellington
1956

Oxford University Press, Amen House, London E.C.4

GLASGOW NEW YORK TORONTO MELBOURNE WELLINGTON
BOMBAY CALCUTTA MADRAS KARACHI CAPE TOWN IBADAN

Geoffrey Cumberlege, Publisher to the University

*

PRINTED IN GREAT BRITAIN
BY THE CAMELOT PRESS LTD.,
LONDON AND SOUTHAMPTON

for N. A. C.

CONTENTS

vii

xiv

ACKNOWLEDGEMENTS

For permission to include their poems in this anthology, we offer our thanks to all the living poets here represented.

Acknowledgement is also made to the Caxton Press for permission to use poems by James K. Baxter, J. C. Beaglehole, James Bertram, Mary Ursula Bethell, Charles Brasch, Allen Curnow, Ruth Dallas, Basil Dowling, A. R. D. Fairburn, Denis Glover, William Hart-Smith, J. R. Hervey, Robin Hyde, M. K. Joseph, R. A. K. Mason, W. H. Oliver, Keith Sinclair, Kendrick Smithyman, Charles Spear and Hubert Witheford; to the Pegasus Press for poems by James K. Baxter, Alistair Campbell, Denis Glover, Louis Johnson, Keith Sinclair, Mary Stanley, Pat Wilson and Hubert Witheford; to A. H. and A. W. Reed for poems by A. R. D. Fairburn, Ruth Gilbert, William Hart-Smith, M. K. Joseph, Keith Sinclair and Anton Vogt; to H. H. Tombs for poems by James Bertram, Ruth Dallas, Ruth Gilbert, W. H. Oliver and Kendrick Smithyman; to the Bulletin Newspaper Company for poems by Hubert Church, J. R. Hervey, D. H. Rogers and Douglas Stewart; to the Progressive Publishing Society for poems by Allen Curnow, Kendrick Smithyman and Anton Vogt; to George Allen and Unwin for poems from Eileen Duggan's *Poems* and *More Poems*, and for a poem by Ruth Gilbert; to the Handcraft Press for poems by Louis Johnson and Kendrick Smithyman; to the Pelorus Press for poems by Kendrick Smithyman and Hubert Witheford; to John Lane The Bodley Head, for poems from D'Arcy Cresswell's *Poems (1924-31)*; to the Lothian Publishing Company for poems by Hubert Church; to the New Zealand University Press for a poem by A. R. D. Fairburn; to the Spearhead Publishers for poems by R. A. K. Mason; to the Unicorn Press of Auckland for poems by D'Arcy Cresswell; to the Richards Press for poems by William Pember Reeves.

The editors of *Landfall*, *The New Zealand Listener*, *Poetry Yearbook*, *New Zealand New Writing*, *Numbers* and *Arena* have given their consent to the inclusion here of certain poems, and this permission we are glad to acknowledge.

To the following literary executors of poets no longer living, our thanks are due for their kind consent to the use of the poems asked for: Dr. Helen Simpson of Christchurch and Laurence Baigent, Esq., of Christchurch, for the late Mary Ursula Bethell; W. R. Edge, Esq., of Auckland, for the late Robin Hyde; Miss G. Mackay, of Christ-church, for the late Jessie Mackay; the Society of Authors and J. Middleton Murry, Esq., O.B.E., for the late Katherine Mansfield; Mrs. Amber Blanco White, of London, for the late William Pember Reeves; and R. D. Rogers, Esq., of Mosgiel, for the late D. H. Rogers.

Poets, publishers, editors and executors have permitted the use of every poem asked for. For this co-operation, and for the generosity of the terms on which the poems have been released, we are deeply grateful.

We wish also to thank the staffs of the Alexander Turnbull Library, Wellington, and the Australian National Library, Canberra, for much help generously given.

Despite extensive inquiries we have failed to trace any holders of copyright on the works of David McKee Wright, William Stenhouse and D. M. Ross. We trust that the persons concerned—and any other holders of copyright whom we may inadvertently have overlooked—will forgive us for the gaps in the above list of acknowledgements. Every effort has been made to complete it.

R. M. C.

J. F. B.

INTRODUCTION

THE last anthology devoted to surveying New Zealand verse from its beginnings appeared in 1906. When that anthology, by Alexander and Currie, was revised and reissued in 1926 it coincided with a turning-point in the development of New Zealand poetry. By far the greater part of the work selected for the present volume has been written since that turning-point, and the question naturally arises: Why is this so in a book planned to present a hundred years of verse? Certainly a century is not long in which to evolve a national literary tradition. We might expect that until a viable literary tradition was established, as it was more or less in the nineteen-thirties, much individual talent would run to waste in a search for direction and form. This is no doubt the short explanation for the hundreds of volumes of dead verses which litter the periods of trial and error. It leaves out of the picture, however, those exceptional writers of nineteenth- and early twentieth-century New Zealand whose poems do survive their time. So, as an introduction to the first part of this anthology, some brief account is required of these successful few and of the trends in verse which they stood for or opposed.

First came men like Barr and Domett. They were Scots and Englishmen preoccupied with the likeness and unlikeness of their fresh experiences to the scenes they knew, the terms of life they had grown up to at home. Browning's friend, Domett, like Broome and Canon Jacobs, was one of the gentleman founders; a colonizing Englishman who returned eventually with his idyll, his 'South Sea Day-Dream', back to a minor place in the literary life of London. Barr is at first glance his opposite. An engineer turned farmer, he celebrated the close community life in the new settlement of the Free Kirk in Otago. Here was no botanizing visitor to a strange physical environment, but rather a settler intent on reflecting in verse the human scene about him. Yet Barr's vision of himself in the role of bard to his community was drawn as directly from the contemporary Burns tradition in Scotland as were the forms of his verse. The gold rushes radically altered the Otago replica of the homeland, and the tradition Barr had transplanted died with the circumstances that had given it meaning.

At least the writing of Barr and Domett has energy and relevance. It is the product of whole men confident of their literary and social background. The rhymers who followed in great numbers had no such advantage. Living most or all of their lives half a world away from London, they met the changing experience and outlook of their countrymen with dreary imitations of the English verse of the time. Publication did not stop; it grew, and the incompetent record of the trappings of overseas poetry was kept up until the first articulate generation of poets, the men of the 'thirties, had been writing for a dozen years.

That there was any worthwhile verse in the barren years was partly a result of the first phase of Australian influence. About 1890, when the New Zealand Government was sending representatives to meetings on Australian federation and when shearers were working first on one and then on the other side of the Tasman Sea, New Zealand authors began to contribute in growing numbers to the Sydney *Bulletin*. This was the period of the consolidation of Australian literary nationalism and the birth of the myth of 'the outback'. The idealized types of the wandering shearers and drovers bore little resemblance to the majority of Australians and even

less to the New Zealand farmer—increasingly a small farmer—
or to the New Zealand townsman. But this Australian movement did have the backing of an authentic balladry to suggest
tone and rhythms for verse, and it did look to its own place
and people so that it showed some relation to the life it was
offering to embody. David McKee Wright is the most notable
and technically-skilled representative of the movement. His
work is lively and it is predominantly honest, though he does
not quite escape the movement's besetting sin of sentimentaliz-
ing what it idealized, a fault which also mars some verse by
Miss B. E. Baughan.

Unfortunately, though perhaps inevitably, the *Bulletin* soon
turned back towards Europe, the *Yellow Book*, and what were
understood to be French symbolism and the lessons of the *fin
de siècle*. Willy nilly, New Zealand writers followed. With one
or two highly individual exceptions they henceforth received
their steadily more outmoded fashions, not at one, but at two
removes from the source. When Pans and dryads, for example,
enjoyed a vogue in Australian verse, 'this fake-pagan Australian art', as A. R. D. Fairburn later observed, 'left imitation
goat-tracks all over New Zealand poetry'. So cramping was
the effect that the decade from 1914 to 1924 was more bare of
creative verse than any since the eighteen-seventies and
'eighties.

Too much weight, however, can be attached to the currents
of the time. The literary environment may explain the rarity
of the more successful writer, just as it circumscribes his style,
but it does not explain his occurrence. William Pember
Reeves, political propagandist, intellectual, Minister of the
Crown, and poet, was in every way exceptional. The stimulus
of analysing and helping to create the new liberal state appears
to have encouraged the expression in poetry of Reeves's vitali-
zing sense of history. He saw the making of New Zealand as a

process with a sweeping, exciting past as well as a future, a past not begun by neighbouring pioneers. In 1896 Reeves took up office as Agent-General for the Colony in London. He wrote little thereafter, though he revised, improved, and privately reissued some of his poems in 1925. As with Wright, who changed with the change in the *Bulletin* and subsequently went to Australia, there was no one to take up Reeves's theme when he abandoned it. His insights were not recovered until the young poets of the 'thirties again looked for their present in the whole panorama of their country's past.

There are a few others. Hubert Church achieved some poetry while attempting a great deal more in model and theme than he was technically able to master. Driven by his sense of personal isolation, religious doubt and melancholy, he built up huge verse discourses in which the Tennyson of *In Memoriam* and the language of Milton are queerly echoed. Jessie Mackay's strength and simplicity of feeling saved something from the medley of influences with which the turn of the century surrounded her. And there are the men of a lucky poem or two: D. H. Rogers, William Stenhouse and, somewhat later, D. M. Ross.

It is against this rarely interrupted story of fruitless borrowing in style and thought that we can appreciate the change that began in the mid-nineteen-twenties and gathered way in the following decade. For two-thirds of a century the writers of verse had been dogged by being neither visitors nor inhabitants. They had looked away from the continual adaptations of their own society and, with slight regard for congruity, had taken the poets of other societies for their models. It can be said in extenuation that it would have been useless to try to express the life of a community that had not found itself. If so, we may regard the fruitful period of New Zealand poetry which followed as a demonstration that conditions had altered by the 'thirties so that it was possible in New Zealand for the artist, in the words of Sir Herbert Read, 'to be insensibly part of an integrated community'.

If this was one factor in producing a truly New Zealand poetry there were certainly others at work also. It would be hard to over-estimate, for instance, the effect of the coming together at Auckland University College of the group who published the magazine *Phoenix* on the students' press in the years 1932 and 1933. The opportunity which was thus provided of publishing poetry independently of the larger printing houses has widened ever since. Robert Lowry and Ronald Holloway, the printers of *Phoenix*, subsequently established presses of their own. Denis Glover, after a visit to the Auckland group, was led to start the Caxton Club Press in Christchurch. This press passed from its student club standing in 1933 and has, over the last twenty years, brought out much of the poetry represented in this anthology.

Besides introducing Allen Curnow, Charles Brasch and James Bertram, the four issues of *Phoenix* presented poems by J. C. Beaglehole, A. R. D. Fairburn and R. A. K. Mason, each of whom had published before. In many ways it was Mason who was the real forerunner of the group. He had published from 1924 onwards a series of small booklets of verse which displayed a sombre personal urgency in a taut metric that owed much to Horace and Housman. Mason's was an individual voice, but the effect of his tense bare verse reinforced an impulse from overseas towards a new style of poetry and a new view of language. This impulse, set going by T. S. Eliot and Ezra Pound some fifteen years before, became in New Zealand another factor which helped liberate, encourage, and set the course for the poetry of the 'thirties.

It would distort the relative importance of the elements which entered into the upsurge of that decade to notice only

xxiii

this last external factor. Its presence, though, raises again a query which our title will have suggested to the reader, namely, What do the words 'New Zealand Verse' mean? To this question the past century has returned successively three different answers. First there was the poetry of Englishmen written in New Zealand. Next came the poetry about New Zealand produced by men divided between two traditions, one distant and exotic, the other in the making. Finally, in the 'thirties, one begins to detect a third and unequivocal answer. For then it became possible to speak of New Zealand poetry as a poetry with which New Zealand patterns of life and thought are fused without effort separate from that of the creative act itself. Time, place and tradition had met.

Can this still be affirmed in the face of the patent influence of overseas writers on the expression of this emerging New Zealand poetry? And why are there no specifically New Zealand verse-forms to present? These frequently-asked questions will be seen to be somewhat deceptive. For they carry an implication that if one claims any distinctness for New Zealand poetry then one is committed to showing a large, even total, distinctness in all sorts of connected fields. Plainly the fact is that what we share with the English-speaking world in general is far more important than the ways in which we differ about living or about art. Our varieties of verse-form are from the common stock of English poetry, a shared stock which in every part of the English-speaking world is fairly constant. And we shared also the problem of finding suitable forms of expression to fit the modern sensibility. This problem, acute after the first World War, was much greater than that involved in modifying the new forms of expression, once found, to suit one of the countries which had participated in the change of sensibility. So, when the poets of the *Phoenix* looked overseas for aid with this major poetic problem of their time, they did not thereby desert or deny their particular function of expressing their own land and community. Only if they had given up the task of modification and fallen back on sterile copying would they have found themselves in the prevailing plight of the preceding sixty years.

Fortunately they took up this function of expressing their land and community without the accompaniment of strident nationalism. Possibly the economic depression helped, by highlighting aspects of New Zealand which would have quietened the most enthusiastic of temperaments. Undoubtedly the writers of the 'twenties accidentally provided a warning by their unassimilated and frequent use of the trivialities of national symbolism to camouflage the derivative nature of their writing. These New Zealand adherents of Georgian and earlier modes also served by charging the newcomers with following degenerate modern poetry from England. Thus the critical skirmishes were fought largely on the subject of technique and this seems to have diverted reviewers from noticing the implicit consciousness of national identity which informed the new poetry. The result was pure gain for the *Phoenix* poets. They recognized a continuing debt to overseas poetry without feeling tempted to try to disguise the fact, while they adapted overseas developments to their own ends and circumstances without being led to assert uniqueness as an aim or to make a doctrine of difference.

Nothing could be easier at this point than to give too strong an impression of the suddenness and completeness of the transition merely by describing and isolating the difference between the false starts of the earlier phases and the solutions approached since. Much was begun before the 'thirties, and afterwards the poetry of Charles Brasch or Denis Glover, of James K. Baxter or Keith Sinclair can very well be viewed as the continuing exploration and extension in poetic terms of what it means to be a New Zealander.

The first emphasis of this exploration was upon landscape and the history of the country. In a poem like Allen Curnow's *Not in Narrow Seas* we can find the themes of William Pember Reeves confirmed, extended and realized. The poetry of Denis Glover and many another selects from the landscape the same significant and increasingly symbolic elements which Domett and Church found there—the gulls, the beaches, the still bush valleys, the unceasing sea. Perhaps we can best see the difference that time has made by comparing the poems about voyages by Domett, D. H. Rogers, and B. E. Baughan with, say, M. K. Joseph's *Mercury Bay Eclogue* or Kendrick Smithyman's *Incident at Matauri*. The long voyage out, sea travel from settlement to settlement, and the ever-present danger of shipwreck, these were the common experience of New Zealand's nineteenth-century immigrants. The present feeling for the sea is different since New Zealanders have established themselves as a coastal people without becoming a notably seafaring one. The alien power of the sea is experienced from its margins, mediated, as it were, through the attitudes of the yachtsman, the fisherman and the holiday-maker.

So also with the view of the land itself. The work of Basil Dowling or Alistair Campbell, for example, expresses a viewpoint consistent with that of a predominantly town-dwelling people with close country relatives and friends, accustomed to touring, hunting and climbing in the not-very-distant fringe where the farming 'back-blocks' merge into the mountains. The natural wildness and magnificence of New Zealand has not been reduced nor its strangeness dissipated. Rather, it has found its place and proportion in the minds of New Zealanders, and this shows in the poetry.

While these themes were being elaborated—as they still are —a second emphasis gradually became apparent. Certain of Allen Curnow's poems, *Stratagem* and *House and Land* for instance, were centred on the people themselves and the flavour of their life. More and more this has become the topic of poetry, particularly since 1943 and 1947 when the periodicals *New Zealand New Writing* and *Landfall* successively introduced a second generation of poets to join the first. These younger poets have inaugurated no departures such as those which marked off the *Phoenix* group from the still-resisting imitators of Edwardian and Georgian models. The two latest generations of writers have been intermingled in style and subject so that Charles Brasch has written both *A View of Rangitoto* and '*I Think of Your Generation*', while Kendrick Smithyman is as truly represented by his poem *The Night Walkers* as by his *Elegy Against a Latter Day*.

If there is consistency there is also variety. Against the pastoral reflective tone of many of the *Phoenix* group may be set the intense personal lyricism of A. R. D. Fairburn. New Zealand is perhaps too small a place to permit a satirist of individuals, but in Fairburn we have also a polished satirist of types. The forceful, acrid poetry of Louis Johnson contrasts as well with the nimble pace of Keith Sinclair as with the static, lacquered set pieces of Charles Spear. A considerable range of technique can be found in the anthology which includes the strict, formal statement of Baxter's *To My Father* and the good-humoured ballad tempo of Dowling's *The Early Days*, the conversational freedom of Hart-Smith's *The Shepherd and the Hawk* and the close-patterned movement of M. K. Joseph's *On the Mountain*. Something of recent symbolism can be discerned in the work of Hubert Witheford and W. H. Oliver, there is something of the idiom of the Kenyon school in the poetry of Kendrick Smithyman, and the influence of Yeats and Dylan Thomas on many will be apparent. At the same time there is sufficient maturity, so much of their own for the writers to say, that they can adapt profitably the forms of variety.

Even so the reader may inquire, Where are the larger poems, political verse, more poems about rural life, perhaps some poetry of the Maoris? It would be as well here to distinguish the absences enforced by principles of selection from those due to a dearth of particular types of poetry in New Zealand.

Shortage of poems of quality about the life of the farmer explains their small showing here. The poets who know this New Zealand, most of them now townsmen, seem to have taken from their early life only a memory of the grand physical backdrop of farming. Perhaps there is something intractable about the material itself, though a deal of New Zealand's finest prose suggests otherwise. And somewhat the same thing can be said of poetry about or by Maoris. No Maori poet has written in English, and the translations have been inadequate to establish communication between the traditions. The late nineteenth century vogue among the colonists for rhymed versions of Maori myths produced only jingling recapitulations of Domett's motif in *Ranolf and Amohia*, or caricatures, with Maori characters, of the saga-telling of contemporary European writers.

In rejecting much work written between 1870 and 1910— for reasons made plain earlier—we reject by the same decisions most of the long poems written in New Zealand. Recent writers seeking to deal with an extended subject have chosen the movement and contrasts of the loose sequence of many short poems of differing form. Even then, three hundred lines usually suffice. Nowhere is the energizing example of a New Zealand poet of genius more obviously missed than in this want of really large and highly developed poems.

One type of verse—the comic—has been under-represented in proportion to its bulk. Rhymesters were constantly poking puns at colonial politicians, and the best of them, Crosbie Ward, had a tidy wit. Unfortunately, Ward, like the rest, took pages to envelop his quarry in a network of quickly-forgotten allusion. Again, in the late 'thirties there was a spring tide of sharp comment in verse on politics and society though little survived at the ebb. Certainly A. R. D. Fairburn and Denis Glover managed to make poetry as well as wry humour in the exercise of their skill at social deflation, so they, with a few others, will be trusted to stand for the transitory many.

We hope that if any other varieties of poem are sought for and not found in the present volume, their absence will also reflect a lack in New Zealand poetry itself. For the aim in selection has been to allow the strengths of New Zealand poetry itself to dictate the balance of the anthology. As it proved, a various, shaped and coherent picture of modern New Zealand and its poetry emerged naturally by keeping to the basis of judging according to the quality of the individual poems. If we felt inclined to lower our standards a little, it was in favour of poets writing before 1924. These isolated craftsmen of our short past compel a measure of respect by the loneliness of their struggle.

The presentation of the rapid development since 1924 has called for careful arrangement. The poems of each poet are presented together and disposed in the order of first publication in magazine or book, unless more direct evidence of the date of composition was available, as it was with Robin Hyde and Kendrick Smithyman. The usual arrangement of poets by date of birth would misrepresent general trends by interspersing among the *Phoenix* generation several writers who began publishing in the 'forties. And an order based on the dates of the poets' first published work, while bringing out technical and thematic progression more clearly, would depend too heavily on whether poets brought out their first work as novices. We have therefore found our order by taking the date of the earliest poem selected from the work of each poet—often more than a book away from his earliest publication—thus obtaining an order which reflects the dates at which the various poets may be said to have 'flourished'.

Inevitably this method also gives a few false directions. D. M. Ross's poem *Bloody Bill* is a vigorous sport from late-*Bulletin*-period stock, and might properly precede R. A. K. Mason's poems. And no method which did not split up the work of Robin Hyde could justly indicate her place in the developing tradition. That place is accidentally less than it might have been because the poem-sequences *The Beaches*, *The Houses* and *The People* were not published for fifteen years after they were written. Had they appeared just before *Journey from New Zealand* (published in December 1938) or *Ku Li* (1940) they might well have speeded up that turning of poetry from the New Zealand scene to New Zealand life which largely followed the end of the second World War. Robin Hyde's poetry anticipated the substance of this change, and indeed its very tone; but the delay in publication which followed her death in 1939 prevented her work from having its immediate effect. This prefiguring of the poetry of the 'forties, however, remains a remarkable individual *tour de force*.

Robin Hyde spent the last year and a half of her life travelling, and most of her contemporaries and many of the latest generation of New Zealand-born writers have spent at least two or three years overseas—usually in England. These visits abroad have not been taken to disqualify a handful of good poems dealing with the experience or produced at the time. The general rule has been to include only the poems of authors who have spent a considerable part of their working life in New Zealand. Barr's poetry appeared after he had been a decade in Otago; Domett's followed upon twenty-eight years and the Premiership of the Colony.

From about the turn of the century the problem becomes principally one of deciding when departing New Zealand poets have lost contact with their country. David McKee Wright went over to Australia in every sense, while Reeves became an academic and business administrator in London. Katherine Mansfield's poems, like her incomparably greater stories, present her as the true exile, emotionally betwixt and between. Only D'Arcy Cresswell has alternated his residence since the 'twenties back and forth from New Zealand to England, and perhaps this is fitting in an important figure of the transitional period of style and associations.

With the 'thirties the poets who leave also return; save for the exception of Douglas Stewart. Unfortunately, the bulk of Stewart's mature and vivid poetry follows by some years his departure and his first two books. His subsequent accomplishment can hardly be regarded as other than Australian. Since the second World War William Hart-Smith has come from Australia to New Zealand. The slowness of the acclimatization of Hart-Smith's talent gives us a measure of the difficulty poets still encounter in making the shift from one variant of the English tradition to another.

To the European onlooker such national, almost regional, differences must appear slight. But the anthology as a whole shows what a delicate and lengthy process is required to give such differences an accurate realization in poetry. To have developed and defined a New Zealand idiom in little more than a hundred years and to have created a body of poetry in that idiom is a not inconsiderable achievement. Yet the anthology displays more than this. The very success of the generation of the 'thirties—their fusing of New Zealand patterns of life and thought with their poetry—has enabled poets here to feel so at ease in their environment that they can simply assume it and find themselves freed to deal directly with the concerns of poetry everywhere.

ROBERT CHAPMAN

1955

HENRY JACOBS

The Avon

Fies nobilium tu quoque fontium.—Horace

I love thee, Avon! though thy banks have known
  No deed of note; thy wand'ring course along
  No bard of Avon hath poured forth in song
Thy tuneful praise; thy modest tide hath flown
For ages on, unheeded and alone.
  I love thee for thy English name, but more
  Because my countrymen along thy shore
Have made new homes. Therefore not all unknown
  Henceforth thy streams shall flow. A little while
Shall see thy wastes grow lovely. Not in vain
  Shall England's sons dwell by thee many a mile.
With verdant meads and fields of waving grain
  Thy rough uncultured banks ere long shall smile;
Heaven-pointing spires shall beautify thy plain.

JOHN BARR OF CRAIGIELEE

There's Nae Place Like Otago Yet

There's nae place like Otago yet,
  There's nae wee beggar weans,
Or auld men shivering at our doors,
  To beg for scraps or banes.
We never see puir working folk
  Wi' bauchles on their feet,
Like perfect icicles wi' cauld,
  Gaun starving through the street.

I

We never hear o' breaking stanes
    A shilling by the yard;
Or poor folk roupit to the door
    To pay the needfu' laird;
Nae purse-proud, upstart, mushroom lord
    To scowl at honest toil,
Or break it down that he, the wretch,
    May feast on roast and boil.

My curse upon them, root and branch,
    A tyrant I abhor;
May despotism's iron foot
    Ne'er mark Otago's shore:
May wealth and labour hand in hand
    Work out our glorious plan,
But never let it be allowed
    That money makes the man.

JOHN BARR OF CRAIGIELEE

The Bonny Harvest Moon

Of all the seasons in the year,
    I like the autumn best,
Ere winter comes with giant strength,
    Or Flora gangs to rest;
When scented breezes fill the air,
    When distant echoes croon,
And ower the hill peeps lazily
    The bonny harvest moon.

2

I like to hear the gentle breeze
    That rustles 'mang the corn,
When Ceres comes with graceful step,
    And waves her crooked horn;
When golden waves sweep o'er the fields,
    When thistles shed their down,
And ower the hill peeps lazily
    The bonny harvest moon.

I like to hear the reapers' sang,
    To me 'tis sweeter far
Than a' the sangs that e'er were sung
    In praise of cruel war;
When brother sheds his brother's blood,
    When despots grasp a croun,
And burning villages obscure
    The bonny harvest moon.

O may sweet peace with gentle sway
    Reign ower Otago's shores,
May beauty smile in every ha',
    While plenty spreads her stores.
May still her boast be honest men,
    And as each year gangs roun',
May grateful hearts rejoice to see
    The bonny harvest moon.

Rise Oot Your Bed

Rise oot your bed, ye worthless wretch,
   The sun's far in the lift,
I never kent a drunken man
   That e'er cam muckle thrift;
See, I've been up since morning grey
   Amang the dirt and weet,
It taks it a', I weel I wat,
   To gar the twa ends meet.

O, woman, will ye haud your tongue,
   My throat is like to crack,
Fling here my breeks, they're at the fire,
   Hung ower the auld chair back.
What time did I come hame yestreen?
   It was a fearfu' nicht;
For Guidsake gie's a nobbler,
   'Twill maybe put me richt.

O weary on your nobblers,
   Your drinking, and your splores,
And weary on your toun exploits,
   Amang your drunken cores.
Ye'll sure be in the newspapers,
   And that ye'll see ere lang,
They needna say Tam Maut is dead
   As lang's ye're fit to gang.

Noo steek your gab, ye've said eneugh,
    And what ye've said's no true,
A pretty pickle ye'd be in
    But for mysel' and pleugh.
Let's see a glass, or haud your tongue,
    I want nane o' your strife,
'Tis pity ye've got sic a man,
    And I've got sic a wife.

And wha's the warst ane o' the twa,
    Ye'll maybe tell me that?
It sets ye weel to lie up there,
    And see me dreepin' wat,
Wi' fechting 'mang the sharney kye,
    'Mang glaur up to the kuits,
Wi' scarce a sark upon my back,
    My taes clean oot my buits.

O swear awa, just swear awa,
    Ye canna bear the truth;
Ye'll what? ye'll rise and tak your nieve
    And gie me ower the mouth:
But, Guidsake, here comes Craigielee,
    Let's a' oor fauts conceal;—
'O come awa, ye're welcome here,
    Our Johnnie's no that weel.'

To My Auld Dog Dash

Puir Dash, thou'rt getting auld and frail,
Nae mair thou wagg'st thy bushy tail,
Whirlin 't aroun' like ony flail,
    About thy rear;
Nae mair thou jump'st ower ditch and rail,
    Like ony deer.

Thou wert the terror o' the kye,
When haflins hid thou used to lie,
Watching the brutes when they cam nigh
    The waving corn;
Or when in stooks it stood to dry,
    When it was shorn.

An honest heart beats in thy breast,
That's something rare 'mang men at least,
Wha look on honour as a jest,
    Or useless folly;
They mair deserve the name o' beast,
    Than thou, puir collie!

But, Dash, if thou could'st only read,
I'd let you see a bonnie screed,
Wad gar ye cock your tail and heid,
    Wi' mickle grace,
How Poet Burns gied dougs their meed,
    And proper place.

The bairns will miss thee when thou'rt dead,
They'll mark the place whaur rests thy heid,
And doun their cheeks the crystal bead
        Will sure distil;
Nae mair wi' them thou'lt tak the lead
        Out ower the hill.

Thou'st had thy time, and thou maun gang,
Whaur days are neither short nor lang;
Nae future joy, nae future pang,
        Hangs o'er thy heid;
Nae fell account for daein' wrang
        Hast thou to dreid.

But dougs and men maun yield to fate,
The gallant heart maun cease to beat;
The humble clown, the lord of state,
        Alike maun gang;
Sae you and I maun tak the gate
        Before it's lang.

JOHN BARR OF CRAIGIELEE

New Zealand Comforts

When to New Zealand first I cam,
    Poor and duddy, poor and duddy,
When to New Zealand first I cam,
    It was a happy day, sirs.
For I was fed on parritch thin,
My taes they stickit thro' my shoon,
I ruggit at the pouken pin,
    But couldna mak it pay, sirs.

7

Baith nicht and day upon the board,
  Ruggin' at it, tuggin' at it,
I strived to please a paper lord,
  Wha ance had been a weaver.
But he got up, and I got doun,
I wandered idly through the toun,
A tattered bonnet on my croon,
  And wasna worth a steever.

Nae mair the laird comes for his rent,
  For his rent, for his rent,
Nae mair the laird comes for his rent,
  When I hae nocht to pay, sirs.
Nae mair he'll tak me aff the loom,
Wi' hanging lip and pouches toom,
To touch my hat, and boo to him,
  The like was never kent, sirs.

But now it's altered days, I trow,
  A weel I wat, a weel I wat,
The beef is tumbling in the pat,
  And I'm baith fat and fu', sirs.
At my door cheeks there's bread and cheese,
I work, or no', just as I please,
I'm fairly settled at my ease,
  And that's the way o't noo, sirs.

ALFRED DOMETT

from Ranolf and Amohia

I

In deep blue sky the sun is bright;
The Port some few miles off in sight;
The pleasant Sea's subsiding swell
Of gales for days gone by may tell,
But on the bar no breaker white,
Only as yet a heavier roll
Denotes where lurks that dangerous shoal.
Alert with lead, and chart, and glass,
The Pilot seeks the well-known pass;
All his familiar marks in view
Together brought, distinct and true.
Erelong the tide's decreasing stream
Chafes at the nearer bank beneath;
The Sea's dark face begins to gleam
(Like tiger roused that shows his teeth)
With many a white foam-streak and seam:
Still should the passage, though more rough,
Have depth of water, width, enough.—
But why, though fair the wind and filled
The sails, though masts and cordage strain,
Why hangs, as by enchantment stilled,
The Ship unmoving?—All in vain
The helm is forced hard down; 'tis plain
The shoal has shifted, and the Ship
Has touched, but o'er its tail, may slip:
She strains—she moves—a moment's bound
She makes ahead—then strikes again
With greater force the harder ground.

9

She broaches to; her broadside black
Full in the breakers' headlong track;
They leap like tigers on their prey;
She rolls as on they come amain,
Rolls heavily as in writhing pain.
The precious time flies fast away—
The launch is swiftly manned and sent
Over the lee, with wild intent
To anchor grapplings where the tide
Runs smoother, and the Ship might ride
Secure beyond the raging bar,
Could they but haul her off so far.
The boat against her bows is smashed;
Beneath the savage surges dashed,
Sucked under by the refluent wave,
They vanish—all those seamen brave.
On—on—the breakers press—no check—
No pause—fly hissing o'er the wreck,
And scour along the dangerous deck.
The bulwarks on the seaward side,
Boats—rudder—sternpost irontied
With deep-driven bolts—how vain a stay!
The weight of waters tears away.
Alas! and nothing can be done—
No downward-hoisted flag—no gun
Be got at to give greater stress
To that unheard demand for aid
By the lost Ship's whole aspect made—
Herself, in piteous helplessness,
One huge sad signal of distress.
Still on—and on—the tide's return
Redoubling now their rage and bulk,
In one fierce sweep from stem to stern

The thundering sheets of breakers roar,
High as the tops in spray-clouds soar,
And down in crashing cataracts pour
Over the rolling, tortured hulk.
Death glares in every horrid shape—
No help—no mercy—no escape!
For falling spars dash out the brains
Of some—and flying guns adrift,
Or splinters crush them—slaughter swift
Whereof no slightest trace remains,
The furious foam no bloodshed stains:
Up to the yards and tops they go—
No hope—no chance of life below!
Then as each ponderous groaning mast
Rocks loosened from its hold at last,
The shrouds and stays, now hanging slack,
Now jerking, bounding, tensely back,
Fling off the helpless victims fast,
Like refuse on the yeast of death
That bellows, raves and boils beneath.
One hapless wretch around his waist
A knotted rope has loosely braced;
When from the stay to which he clings,
The jerking mast the doomed one flings,
It slips—and by the neck he swings:
Death grins and glares in hideous shape—
No hope—no pity—no escape!—
Still on and on—all day the same,
Through all that brilliant summer day
Beneath a sky so blithe and blue
The wild white whirl of waters flew,
In stunning vollies overswept
And beat the black Ship's yielding frame. . . .

Still on—still on—like fiends of Hell
Whiter than Angels—frantic—fell,
Through all that summer day the same
The merciless murderous breakers came!
And to the mizen-top that swayed
With every breach those breakers made,
Unaided, impotent to aid—
The mates and Master clung all day.
There—while the Sun onlooking gay
Triumphant trod his bright highway;
There, till his cloudless rich decline—
Faint in the blinding deafening drench
Of salt waves roaring down the whine
And creaking groans each grinding wrench
Took from the tortured timbers—there
All day—all day—in their despair,
The gently brave, the roughly good,
Collected, calm and silent stood.

And now the foam spurts up between
The starting deck-planks; downward bowed
The mighty masts terrific lean;
Then each with its despairing crowd
Of life, with one tremendous roar
Falls like a tower—and all is o'er.

II

And Tangi and his tribe thus much had gained,
Those vices lost, but all their gods retained.
A love of change was never fault of his,
And least he fancied such a change as this.
Once when a zealous teacher from the North
The terrors of his creed had thundered forth—

Unfolded with keen zest and kind desire
To save his hearers from so sad a fate,
His pleasant faith in everlasting fire,
And painted all the pangs the damned await—
While horror blanched the cheeks of half the crowd,
Old Tangi roared with laughter long and loud:
That Hell of theirs, he said, might be a place
Wholesome and fitting for the white man's race,
No Maori was half bad enough to be
Doomed to so horrible a destiny:
Had a good Spirit destined for such woe
His children after death, he long ago
Had sent some trusty friend to let them know;
But he for his part would have nought to do
With any *Atua*, whether false or true,
Who could delight his direst foe to see
The victim of such monstrous cruelty.
And when he learnt what adverse sects prevailed
And how each other's doctrines they assailed,
He held his hand out, with the fingers spread—
'So many ways to heaven you teach,' he said;
'When you have fixed the right one and none doubt it,
'Twill then be time for *me* to think about it.'

III

Or to the beach descending, with joined hands
They pace the firm tide-saturated sands
Whitening beneath their footpress as they pass;
And from that fresh and tender marble floor
So glossy-shining in the morning sun,
Watch the broad billows at their chase untiring—
How they come rolling on, in rougher weather—
How in long lines they swell and link together,

Till, as their watery walls they grandly lift,
Their level crests extending sideways, swift
Shoot over into headlong roofs of glass
Cylindric—thundering as they curl and run
And close, down-rushing to a weltering dance
Of foam that slides along the smooth expanse,
Nor seldom, in a streaked and creamy sheet
Comes unexpected hissing round their feet,
While with great leaps and hurry-scurry fleet,
His louder laughter mixed with hers so sweet,
Each tries to stop the other's quick retreat.
Or else on sands that, white and loose, give way
At every step, they toil; till labor-sped
Their limbs in the noon-loneliness they lay
On that hot, soft, yet unelastic bed,
With brittle seaweed, pink and black o'erstrewn,
And wrecks of many a forest-growth upthrown,
Bare stem and barkless branches, clean, sea-bleached,
Milk-white—or stringy logs deep-red as wine,
Their ends ground smooth against a thousand rocks,
Dead-heavy, soaked with penetrating brine;
Or bolted fragment of some Ship storm-breached
And shattered—all with barnacles o'ergrown,
Grey-crusted thick with hollow-coned small shells—
So silent in the sunshine still and lone,
So reticent of what it sadly tells. . . .

IV

And near some river-mouth—shoal—marshy-wide—
Would mark the swarming sea-birds o'er the waste
Tremble across the air in glimmering flocks;
Or how, long-legged, with little steps they plied
Their yellow webs, in such high-shouldered haste

Pattering along the cockle-filled sandbanks,
Some refuse dainty of the Sea to taste;
Or standing stupefied in huddled ranks
Still rounded up by the advancing tide—
White glittering squadrons on the level mud
Dressing their lines before the enclosing flood. . . .

v

So Ranolf felt when over wood and wild
That quiet sadness first began to creep;
And sheltered safe within their mountain-nook
On his fern-pillow he could lie and look
Past forest tree-tops surging down the steep,
With rocks out-slanting bold, dark-red and grey—
Through the glen's mouth, o'er yellow plains outside,
Mixed with the skies, it seemed, so high and wide—
Melting to misty dimness far away;—
Look—but to feel with more supreme content
That luxury of loneliness profound—
No human soul but theirs for miles around!
Feel how serenely, pensively forlorn
The tender silence of the tearful Morn;
Of those unmoving trees as still as thought,
And leaves imbibing in their happy sleep
Rich greenness ever more refreshed and deep;
Each branch with bright drops hung that would not fall
The faint blue haze upon the grass; while nought
But the slight tremble, shimmering on the shade
So glowing dark about their stems, betrayed
The fine soft rain's inaudible descent.

Then, as the thickening weather with its pall
Of gloom shut out the distant hills and sky,
How pleasant there to lounge secure and mark
Emerging from the mists in forests high
Black jutting trees to shadows turn, and fade,
Where sullen, ragged, smothering vapors weighed
Upon the nearer summits. . . .

VI

But Evening now
Steals, like a serious thought o'er joyous face,
Its cooling veil o'er the warm Earth to throw.
The hawk no longer soars in pride of place,
Stiff-wheeling with bent head in circles slow;
The teal and wild-duck leave the floating weed
And open pool, for sheltering rush and reed;
And home with outstretched necks the cormorants fly
In strings—each train dark-lettering the sky,
Now V exact, now lengthening into Y—
As arrow-like direct their course they steer
To haunts afar, unseen, but somewhere near
Those mountain-summits carpeted and black
With forests dense without a break or track,
Whence smooth and ferny spurs in golden dun
Of solemn sunlight undulating run
Down to dim bases lost in shadows blue
That blot the intervening gullies too—
Encroaching darkness creeping upward still
O'er chequered black-and-gold of dell and hill.

VII

About the heights, soft clouds, a few,
Clung here and there like floating flue;
Like helpless sea-birds breeze-bereft,
Unmoving spread their pinions white—
From jutting crag, deep-bathed in light,
To slip away in snowy flight;
Or closely crouched in shadowy cleft,
Like lambing ewes the flock has left.
Below, o'erjoyed at darkness fleeing,
Reviving Nature woke again
To all the exceeding bliss of being!
The minnows leapt the liquid plain
In shoals—each silvery-shivering train,
A sudden dash of sprinkled rain!
The wild-ducks' black and tiny fleet
Shot in-and-out their shy retreat;
The cormorant left his crowded tree
And stretched his tinselled neck for sea;
All Nature's feathered favourites poured
To their adored undoubted Lord
Of light and heat, accordance sweet. . . .

FREDERICK NAPIER BROOME

A Leave-taking

The seamen shout once and together,
    The anchor breaks up from the ground,
And the ship's head swings to the weather,
    To the wind and the sea swings round:

With a clamour the great sail steadies,
  In extreme of a storm scarce furled;
Already a short wake eddies,
  And a furrow is cleft and curled
    To the right and left.

Float out from the harbour and highland
  That hides all the region I know,
Let me look a last time on the island
  Well seen from the sea to the snow.
The lines of the ranges I follow,
  I travel the hills with my eyes,
For I know where they make a deep hollow,
  A valley of grass and the rise
    Of streams clearer than glass.

Now my days leave the soft silent byway,
  And clothed in a various sort,
In iron or gold, on the highway
  New feet shall succeed, or stop short:
Shod hard these may be, or made splendid,
  Fair and many, or evil and few,
But the going of bare feet has ended,
  Of naked feet set in the new
    Meadow grass sweet and wet.

I will long for the ways of soft walking,
  Grown tired of the dust and the glare,
And mute in the midst of much talking,
  Will pine for the silences rare;
Streets of peril and speech full of malice
  Will recall me the pastures and peace
Which gardened and guarded those valleys
  With grasses as high as the knees,
    Calm as high as the sky.

A singing place fitter than vessel
    Cold winds draw away to the sea,
Where many birds flutter and nestle
    And come near and wonder at me,
Where the bell-bird sets solitudes ringing:
    Many times I have heard and thrown down
My lyre in despair of all singing;
    For things lovely what word is a crown
        Like the song of a bird?

For the island secure in my spirit
    At ease on its own ocean rides,
And Memory, a ship sailing near it,
    Shall float in with favouring tides,
Shall enter the harbours and land me
    To visit the gorges and heights
Whose aspects seemed once to command me,
    As queens by their charms command knights
        To achievements of arms.

The last of her now is a brightening
    Far fire in the forested hills,
The breeze as the night nears is heightening,
    The cordage draws tighter and thrills,
Like a horse that is spurred by the rider,
    The great vessel quivers and quails,
And passes the billows beside her,
    The fair wind is strong in her sails,
        She is lifted along.

When the zone and the latitude changes
    A welcome of white cliffs shall be,
I shall cease to be sad for white ranges
    Now lost in the night and the sea:—

But dipped deep in their clear flowing rivers
   As a chalice my spirit shall weigh
With fair water that flickers and shivers,
   Held up to the strong, steady ray,
      To the sunlight of song.

JESSIE MACKAY

Maisrie

Maisrie sits in the Gled's Nest Tower,
   A' her lane in the fine June weather.
The wind steals up an' the wind wins owre,
   An' its sang is 'O for the wild west heather,
      Maisrie, Maisrie!

'O hae ye mind o' blue Loch Linn
   That rocked ye to sleep, the bairn o' the shieling?
An' hae ye mind o' the sea-mews' din
   When the sun dips red an' they're hameward wheeling,
      Maisrie, Maisrie?

'Hae ye forgotten the Yule by the sea,
   Maisrie o' Linn, before ye were Lady?
The dance to the pipes an' the lilting free,
   An' your ain heart licht under Highland plaidie,
      Maisrie, Maisrie?

'O hae ye mind o' the fisher-folk
   That lo'ed an' tined ye because ye were bonnie?
The hame hearth-stane wi' its bleeze an' smoke,
   An' the mither that held ye dearest of ony,
      Maisrie, Maisrie?

'Or hae ye forgotten great Ben Mhor,
   His cleft black heid whaur storm-reeks gather;
The snaw-wings faulding him hind an' fore?
   Wad ye your garden o' roses rather,
               Maisrie, Maisrie?'

Maisrie looks owre park an' hind;
   But her thochts are far when nicht is fa'ing:—
'A waefu' sough has the dowie wind,
   That comes to me as an owlet ca'ing
               "Maisrie, Maisrie."

'Siller is bricht an' pearls are fine;
   But the shells o' Loch Linn to me were dearer:
An' o' a' the lilts I hae heard sin syne
   The fisherman's voice sang aye the clearer
               "Lost Lady Maisrie!"

'An' I hae mind o' great Ben Mhor,
   That I an' my sisters climbed thegither;
For ae look o' his drifting hoar
   My garden of roses fast might wither
               An' dee, for Maisrie!

'She sighs frae the kirkyaird by the sea—
   My mither, that lies by the rowan shady—
"There's rest, bonnie bairnie, here wi' me,
   For the fisher-wife an' the weary lady,
               Maisrie, Maisrie!" '

JESSIE MACKAY

For Love of Appin

The hand is to the plough an' the e'e is to the trail;
The river-boatie dances wi' her heid to the gale;
 But she'll never ride to Appin;
 We'll see nae mair o' Appin,
For ye ken we crooned 'Lochaber' at the saut sea's gate.
 It's a land o' giantrie;
 Its lochs are like the sea:
 But it's no a desert fairly;
 The corn's fu' an' early;
 Ye'll hear the laddies daffing;
 Ye'll hear the lassies laughing;
 But we—we canna tine
 What lies ayont the brine:
 When we sang 'Lochaber' then
 We were gray, gray men.
 We'll smile nae mair for ever
 By the prairie or the river,
 Lest ony think perchance that we forget
 The rainy road to Appin,—
 East awa' to Appin,—
The rainy road to Appin that the leal men went.

They tore us oot o' Scotland, they flang us in the west
Like a bairn's thread o' beads, an' we downa look for rest,
 But it's O to lie in Appin,—
 I' the haly sod o' Appin,—
It's O to lie in Appin where the mist haps a'!
 Cauld is this to live or die on,
 But we brought the tents o' Zion;

An' weel the mark is seen
Where the martyr-blood hath been
That will clear us to the Lord
When the Angel wi' the sword
Gangs nightly up the land
O' an Egypt that is banned.
But God do sae an' mair
To us, gin we cast a care,
Or smile again for ever
By the prairie or the river,
Lest ony think perchance that we forget
The red road to Appin,—
East awa' to Appin,—
The red road to Appin that the heart's blood tracked!

It's no a desert fairly, it's grand an' young an' fine;
Here the sons o' Anak might live an' press the wine;
But it's O for hame an' Appin,
The heather hills o' Appin,—
The thousand years o' Appin where the leal men lie!
Oor face is set as stane,
But we'll thank the Lord again,—
Gang saftly a' oor days;
An' wark shall be oor praise.
The bairns will tak' a root
By the mighty mountain foot;
But we—we canna sever;
It's no for us whatever;
We hear nae earthly singing
But it sets 'Lochaber' ringing.
An' we'll never smile again
I' the sunlight or the rain

Till oor feet are on the lang last trail,—
  The siller road to Appin,—
  East awa' to Appin,—
The siller road to Appin rinnin' a' the way to God!

JESSIE MACKAY

The Burial of Sir John McKenzie

They played him home to the House of Stones,
  All the way, all the way,
To his grave in the sound of the winter sea.
  The sky was dour, the sky was gray.
They played him home with the chieftain's dirge
Till the wail was wed to the rolling surge!
They played him home with a sorrowful will
To his grave at the foot of the Holy Hill;
  And the pipes went mourning all the way.

Strong hands that struck for right
  All the day, all the day,
Folded now in the dark of earth—
  The veiled dawn of the upper way!
Strong hands that struck with his
From days that were to the day that is
Carry him now from the house of woe
To ride the way the Chief must go;
  And his peers went mourning all the way.

Son and brother, at his right hand
  All the way, all the way!
And O for them and O for her
  Who stayed within, the dowie day!

Son and brother and near of kin
Go out with the Chief who never comes in!
And of all who loved him far and near
'Twas the nearest most that held him dear;
　　And his kin went mourning all the way.

The clan went on with the pipes before
　　All the way, all the way;
A wider clan than ever he knew
　　Followed him home that dowie day.
And who were they of the wider clan?
The landless man and the No Man's man,
The man that lacked and the man unlearned,
The man that lived but as he earned;
　　And the clan went mourning all the way.

The heart of New Zealand went beside
　　All the way, all the way,
To the resting-place of her Highland chief;
　　Much she thought she could not say.
He found her a land of many domains,
Maiden forest and fallow plains:
He left her a land of many homes,—
The pearl of the world where the sea-wind roams;
　　And New Zealand went mourning all the way!

In Galilee

Herod the King came sounding through
Capernaum gate with a revelling crew;
Beyond his garden of sycophants,
He saw but a thousand crawling ants.

Judas the Mammonite masked his heart
With a crooked smile in Capernaum mart,—
And up the street as he went his way,
He saw but a thousand masks of clay.

John the Dreamer walked up and down
The streets of old Capernaum town;
And naught he saw with his raptured eye
But a thousand phantoms hurrying by.

Soft as snow to Capernaum drew
Jesus the Christ, and no man knew.
He saw as in a painted scroll
The ant, the mask, and the phantom soul.

But in and over and back of them all,
He saw, by old Capernaum wall,
The angel of each to whom was given
To stand before their God in Heaven.

WILLIAM PEMBER REEVES

Nox Benigna

How kind is night
After the fierceness of the summer day,
That glared so long on yellow grass and gray
And earth-cracks parted as parched lips that pray
    For water bright!

How wide the calm!
The endless, fading plain, how white and still,
How black the pines against the moonlit hill,
How loud has grown the little thread of rill
    Beside yon palm!

Beneath the range
Deep shadows lurk behind a silver screen
In thick, hot air, the clustering trunks between.
The wild-bird's note within the dark ravine
    Calls clear and strange.

The wind awakes,
And over distant mountains grassy, dry,
Blown by its breath the red fires leap and fly,
Or, climbing backward, slowly creep on high,
    Thin golden snakes.

Now ceases pain.
The myriad brittle straws that make life's sheaf,
The needle-pricks more hard to bear than grief,
Are gone as dust is washed from off the leaf
    When comes the rain.

WILLIAM PEMBER REEVES

The Passing of the Forest

All glory cannot vanish from the hills.
   Their strength remains, their stature of command
O'er shadowy valleys that cool twilight fills
   For wanderers weary in a faded land;
Refreshed when rain-clouds swell a thousand rills,
   Ancient of days in green old age they stand,
Though lost the beauty that became Man's prey
When from their flanks he stripped the woods away.

But thin their vesture now—the trembling grass
   Shivering and yielding as the breeze goes by,
Catching quick gleams and scudding shades that pass
   As running seas reflect a windy sky.
A kinglier garb their forest raiment was
   From crown to feet that clothed them royally,
Shielding the secrets of their streams from day
Ere the deep, sheltering woods were hewn away.

Well may these brooding, mutilated kings,
   Stripped of the robes that ages weaved, discrowned,
Draw down the clouds with soft-enfolding wings
   And white, aerial fleece to wrap them round,
To hide the scars that every season brings,
   The fire's black smirch, the landslip's gaping wound,
Well may they shroud their heads in mantle grey
Since from their brows the leaves were plucked away!

Gone is the forest's labyrinth of life,
    Its clambering, thrusting, clasping, throttling race,
Creeper with creeper, bush with bush at strife,
    Struggling in silence for a breathing space;
Below, a realm with tangled rankness rife,
    Aloft, tree columns in victorious grace.
Gone the dumb hosts in warfare dim; none stay;
Dense brake and stately trunk have passed away.

Gone are those gentle forest-haunting things,
    Eaters of honey, honey-sweet in song.
The tui and the bell-bird—he who rings
    That brief, rich music we would fain prolong,
Gone the woodpigeon's sudden whirr of wings,
    The daring robin all unused to wrong,
Ay, all the friendly friendless creatures. They
Lived with their trees and died and passed away.

Gone are the flowers. The kowhai like ripe corn,
    The frail convolvulus, a day-dream white,
And dim-hued passion-flowers for shadows born,
    Wan orchids strange as ghosts of tropic night;
The blood-red rata strangling trees forlorn
    Or with exultant scarlet fiery bright
Painting the sombre gorges, and that fay
The starry clematis are all away!

Lost is the resinous, sharp scent of pines,
    Of wood fresh cut, clean-smelling for the hearth,
Of smoke from burning logs in wavering lines
    Softening the air with blue, of brown, damp earth

And dead trunks fallen among coiling vines,
    Slow-mouldering, moss-coated. Round the girth
Of the green land the wind brought vale and bay
Fragrance far-borne now faded all away.

Lost is the sense of noiseless sweet escape
    From dust of stony plain, from sun and gale,
When the feet tread where quiet shadows drape
    Dark stems with peace beneath a kindly veil.
No more the pleasant rustlings stir each shape,
    Creeping with whisperings that rise and fail
Through glimmering lace-work lit by chequered play
Of light that danced on moss now burned away.

Gone are the forest tracks, where oft we rode
    Under the silver fern-fronds climbing slow,
In cool, green tunnels, though fierce noontide glowed
    And glittered on the tree-tops far below.
There, 'mid the stillness of the mountain road,
    We just could hear the valley river flow,
Whose voice through many a windless summer day
Haunted the silent woods, now passed away.

Drinking fresh odours, spicy wafts that blew,
    We watched the glassy, quivering air asleep,
Midway between tall cliffs that taller grew
    Above the unseen torrent calling deep;
Till, like a sword, cleaving the foliage through,
    The waterfall flashed foaming down the steep:
White, living water, cooling with its spray
Dense plumes of fragile fern, now scorched away.

The axe bites deep. The rushing fire streams bright;
   Swift, beautiful and fierce it speeds for Man,
Nature's rough-handed foeman, keen to smite
   And mar the loveliness of ages. Scan
The blackened forest ruined in a night,
   The sylvan Parthenon that God will plan
But builds not twice. Ah, bitter price to pay
For Man's dominion—beauty swept away!

WILLIAM PEMBER REEVES

The Albatross

Yet through the turmoil comfortless and loud,
Welter and yeast of sea-wash, gust and cloud,
The clamour, yet monotony of storm,
One shape disdainful, gravely-speeding form
Was ever tranquil on the tempest's wing—
The albatross, the Southern Ocean's king,
Whose billow-shaken, wind-tormented throne
Looks from the portals of the White Unknown
Out o'er the salt, earth-girdling waste; whose flight
Is beauty's self, so grace and strength unite.
See the great bird with easy, gliding sweep,
Outstrip the swiftest sailer of the deep!
Or 'gainst the gale with few slow beats prevailing
And power not half expended yet availing!
Or balancing on stiffened pinions there
He floats as calmly on the frantic air
As white swan dreaming by a river-nest,—
Yea, takes upon the storm-wind's back his rest

With wide-extended steadfast wings displayed
Curved with the cruel grace of Eastern blade.
Then glancing sidelong o'er the wave-tops shows
Full rounded breast and spread of wings—their snows
And all their ample span—and seems to graze
Yet brushes not the hissing, flying sprays,
Spirit of speed aërial! Now he dips
Into wild pits of death his pinion-tips,
Then upward veers, captures the wind's whole might,
And rushing with the tempest finds the night.

WILLIAM PEMBER REEVES

The Dutch Seamen and New Holland

Southward and eastward had our seamen steered
And borne back tales of lands hot, arid, feared.
League upon league their patient ships had won,
Yet southward aye the wilderness stretched on
Lonely and dead as by enchantment doomed.
Oft through the haze dim yellow headlands loomed
Fronting the deep with tawny monstrous shapes,
Fantastic bulwarks, man-like, bird-like capes.
Seldom the sound of streams awoke the strand,
For God's good rain had half forgot the land.
Only the loud cicala, tireless, shrill,
Jarred 'mid the leaves on every sunburnt hill;
And beasts grotesquely leaping, harmless, shy,
Fled at a voice or blundered careless by;
And, buzzing, loathèd plague to ears and eyes,
Came, swarms of hate, black countless ceaseless flies.

So when in need of water or of wood
Our sailors on the silent beaches stood,
And at their feet the hot sand glowed and gleamed,
And o'er their heads the uncaring heaven dreamed,
Awestruck they swore the solemn shore was cursed,
Bound by dread spells of silence, heat, and thirst.
Nor found they sign in cave, on rock or hill,
Of craft of man or kindly human skill,
Save certain booths they chanced on by the shore—
Stakes slanted, boughs set endwise, nothing more,
Half a babe's castle, half a wild brute's lair,
Rude, childish, pitiful: and lurking there,
Beyond the trees, gaunt stealthy forms sped far,
And long, wild cries seemed shouts of fear and war.

WILLIAM PEMBER REEVES

A Colonist in His Garden

He reads a letter

'Dim grows your face, and in my ears,
Filled with the tramp of hurrying years,
   Your voice dies, far apart.
Our shortening day draws in, alack!
Old Friend, ere darkness falls, turn back
   To England, life and art.

'Write not that you content can be,
Pent by that drear and shipless sea
   Round lonely islands rolled,
Isles nigh as empty as their deep,
Where men but talk of gold and sheep
   And think of sheep and gold.

'A land without a past; a race
Set in the rut of commonplace;
  Where Demos overfed
Allows no gulf, respects no height;
And grace and colour, music, light,
  From sturdy scorn are fled.

'I'll draw you home. Lo! As I write
A flash—a swallow's arrow-flight!
  O'erhead the skylark's wings
Quiver with joy at winter's rout:
A gust of April from without
  Scents of the garden brings.

'The quickening turf is starred with gold;
The orchard wall, rust-red and old,
  Glows in the sunlight long.
The very yew-tree warms to-day,
As the sundial, mossed and grey,
  Marks with a shadow strong.

'Tired of the bold aggressive New,
Say, will your eyes not joy to view,
  In a sedater clime,
How mellowing tones at leisure steal,
And age hath virtue scars to heal,
  And beauty weds grey Time?'

He speaks

Good wizard! Thus he weaves his spell.
Yet, charm he twenty times as well,
  Me shall he never spur,
To seek again the old, green land,
That seems from far to stretch a hand
  To sons who dream of her.

34

For is my England there? Ah, no.
Gone is my England, long ago,
    Leaving me tender joys,
Sweet unforgotten fragrance, names
Of wrinkled men and grey-haired dames,
    To me still girls and boys.

With these in youth let memory stray
In pleasance green, where stern to-day
    Works Fancy no mischance.
Dear pleasance—let no light invade
Revealing ravage Time hath made
    Amid thy dim romance!

Here am I rooted. Firm and fast
We men take root who face the blast,
    When to the desert come,
We stand where none before have stood
And braving tempest, drought and flood,
    Fight Nature for a home.

Now, when the fight is o'er, what man
What wrestler, who in manhood's span
    Hath won so stern a fall,
Who, matched against the desert's power,
Hath made the wilderness to flower,
    Can turn, forsaking all?

Yet that my heart to England cleaves
This garden tells with blooms and leaves
    In old familiar throng,
And smells, sweet English, every one,
And English turf to tread upon,
    And English blackbird's song.

'No art?' Who serve an art more great
Than we, rough architects of State
   With the old Earth at strife?
'No colour?' On the silent waste
In pigments not to be effaced,
   We paint the hues of life.

'A land without a past?' Nay, nay.
I saw it, forty years this day.
   —Nor man, nor beast, nor tree.
Wide, empty plains where shadows pass
Blown by the wind o'er whispering grass
   Whose sigh crept after me.

Now when at midnight round my doors
The gale through sheltering branches roars,
   What is it to the might
Of the mad gorge-wind that o'erthrew
My camp—the first I pitched—and blew
   Our tents into the night?

Mine is the vista where the blue
And white-capped mountains close the view.
   Each tapering cypress there
At planting in these hands was borne,
Small, shivering seedlings and forlorn,
   When all the plain was bare!

Skies, without music, mute through time,
Now hear the skylark's rippling climb
   Challenge their loftier dome.
And hark! A song of gardens floats,
Rills, gushes clear—the self-same notes
   Your thrushes flute at Home.

See, I have poured o'er plain and hill
Gold open-handed, wealth that will
   Win children's children's smiles,
—Autumnal glories, glowing leaves,
And aureate flowers, and warmth of sheaves,
   Mid weary pastoral miles.

Yonder my poplars, burning gold,
Flare in tall rows of torches bold,
   Spire beyond kindling spire.
Then raining gold round silver stem
Soft birches gleam. Outflaming them
   My oaks take ruddier fire.

And with my flowers about her spread
(None brighter than her shining head),
   The lady of my close,
My daughter, walks in girlhood fair.
Friend, could I rear in England's air
   A sweeter English rose?

DAVID McKEE WRIGHT

The Duff

It was on a Sunday morning, the church was far away,
They used to keep the Sabbath in their own up-country way—
They washed their clothes and darned their socks and smoked
   a lot all day.
Says Jack M'Kay to Billy Barnes—'Look here, old mate,'
   says he,
'I'll cook the spuds and roast the meat and make a drink of tea,
And you can build a duff!' 'All right, old mate,' says he,
'And good enough.'

It was a warmish kind of day, the fire was brightish too;
He minced the suet very fine and shoved the currants
through
According to a recipe that told him what to do.
Says Billy Barnes to Jack M'Kay—'Look here, old mate,'
says he,
'This'll be something like a feed, and you can trust to me
For something like a duff!' 'All right, old mate,' says he,
'And good enough.'

The spuds and meat were nicely done, the billy tea was
made,
With plates and bright tin pannikins the whisky-case was
laid—
They should have left that duff alone to them that's learned
their trade.
Says Jack M'Kay to Billy Barnes—'Look here, old mate,'
says he,
'That pot's been boiling long enough, just hook him off and
see
How goes the blooming duff!' 'All right, old mate,' says he,
'And good enough.'

They got the pot hooked off the fire, they looked with curious
eyes
As from the vessel's sooty rim they saw the monster rise—
Whatever else was wrong with it they must repect its *size*.
Says Billy Barnes to Jack M'Kay—'Look here, old mate,'
says he,
'It's pretty heavy on my arm, but just you wait and see—
It's me can build a duff!' 'All right, old mate,' says he,
'And good enough.'

38

They cut the string that bound the cloth and let the wonder
  go;
It didn't jump about like mad nor yet begin to flow,
As other duffs are known to do, but just lay smiling low.
Says Jack M'Kay to Billy Barnes—'Look here, old mate,'
  says he,
'It looks about as rum a thing as ever yet I see;
Still—I suppose it's duff!' 'You bet, old mate,' says he,
'And good enough.'

They let it stand a little while and tackled on the meat,
With just a stray look now and then to see it kept its seat—
They both were half afraid of it, but neither would be beat.
Says Billy Barnes to Jack M'Kay—'Look here, old mate,'
  says he,
'Let's cut the rummy thing in half and tackle some and see
If it is blooming duff.' 'All right, old mate,' says he,
'And good enough.'

It tasted something like a stew of sweepings of a store—
Tobacco, nutmeg, candles, glue, and flavourings galore—
So wonderful a kind of taste was never known before!
Says Jack M'Kay to Billy Barnes—'Look here, old mate,'
  says he,
'The flavour of this blooming thing can't well be drowned in
  tea—
Let's leave the blooming duff!' 'All right, old mate,' says he,
'And good enough.'

That evening from a lonely pub the two mates started back,
The creeks were roaring pretty high along the barren track,
They'd had a lot of whisky hot, the night was pretty black!

Says Billy Barnes to Jack M'Kay—'Look here, old mate,' says he,
'The creek and river's up a bit and hanged if I can see—
It's all that blooming duff.' 'Hold up, old mate,' says he,
'You're right enough.'

They reached the river rolling wide, they had to wade the
    stream,
And spite of all the whisky it was colder than ice-cream;
And Bill was thinking as he went the duff would make him
    dream.
Says Jack M'Kay to Billy Barnes—'Look here, old mate,'
    says he,
'I'm sinking in a blooming hole, you'd best let go of me—
It's all that cursed duff!' 'I'm sinking too,' says he,
'And fast enough.'

DAVID McKEE WRIGHT

While the Billy Boils

The speargrass crackles under the billy and overhead is the
    winter sun;
There's snow on the hills, there's frost in the gully, that minds
    me of things that I've seen and done,
Of blokes that I knew, and mates that I've worked with, and
    the sprees we had in the days gone by;
And a mist comes up from my heart to my eyelids, I feel fair
    sick and I wonder why.

There is coves and coves! Some I liked partic'lar, and some
    I would sooner I never knowed;
But a bloke can't choose the chaps that he's thrown with in
    the harvest paddock or here on the road.

40

There was chaps from the other side that I shore with that
    I'd like to have taken along for mates,
But we said, 'So long!' and we laughed and parted for good
    and all at the station gates.

I mind the time when the snow was drifting and Billy and me
    was out for the night—
We lay in the lee of a rock, and waited, hungry and cold, for
    the morning light.
Then he went one way and I the other—we'd been like
    brothers for half a year;
He said: 'I'll see you again in town, mate, and we'll blow the
    froth off a pint of beer.'

He went to a job on the plain he knowed of and I went poison-
    ing out at the back,
And I missed him somehow—for all my looking I never could
    knock across his track.
The same with Harry, the bloke I worked with the time I was
    over upon the Coast,
He went for a fly-round over to Sydney, to stay for a fortnight
    —a month at most!

He never came back, and he never wrote me—I wonder how
    blokes like him forget;
We had been where no one had been before us, we had
    starved for days in the cold and wet;
We had sunk a hundred holes that was duffers, till at last we
    came on a fairish patch,
And we worked in rags in the dead of winter while the ice
    bars hung from the frozen thatch.

Yes, them was two, and I can't help mind them—good mates
    as ever a joker had;
But there's plenty more as I'd like to be with, for half of the
    blokes on the road is bad.
It sets me a-thinking the world seems wider, for all we fancy
    it's middling small,
When a chap like me makes friends in plenty and they slip
    away and he loses them all.

The speargrass crackles under the billy and overhead is the
    winter sun;
There's snow on the hills, there's frost in the gully, and, Oh,
    the things that I've seen and done,
The blokes that I knowed and the mates I've worked with, and
    the sprees we had in the days gone by;
But I somehow fancy we'll all be pen-mates on the day when
    they call the Roll of the Sky.

DAVID McKEE WRIGHT

Arlington

The sun shines bright on Arlington, the drowsy sheep creep
    by,
The water races seam the hills, cloud shadows line the sky,
New fences climb the warm brown spurs to guard the scrubber
    ewes,
Because the run is broken up for hungry cockatoos.
The township sleeps below the hill, the homestead on the
    plain,
But the lost days of Arlington will never come again.

The working men are seen no more in hut or rabbit camp,
The stockwhip never will be heard about the river swamp,
No more the mighty fleeces crown the bins like drifted snow,
No more the princely rams go down, the wonder of the show;
The swagger on the weary tramp comes o'er the summer
    plain,
And sighs for rest at Arlington, yet knows he sighs in vain.

There's little work on Arlington since the old station days;
The hawk-faced owners groan to tell sheep-farming never
    pays,
They build no homesteads on the runs, they pay no wages out;
The station style was different when money flew about.
The rabbits flourish on the hills and burrow all the plain,
The stock that ran on Arlington will never run again.

The good old boss of Arlington was everybody's friend,
He liked to keep the wages up right to the very end;
If diggers' horses went astray they always could be found,
The cow that roamed across the run was never in the pound.
He was a white man through and through, cheery and fair
    and plain,
And now he'll never ride the rounds of Arlington again.

And yet the talk is evermore, 'The people want the land!'
I tell you that the workers' cry is, 'Let the stations stand.'
The greedy few will clamour loud and clamour to the end;
A dummy grabbing what he can is not the people's friend.
And Heaven's curse is on him still in all his schemes for gain;
He falls—and yet old Arlington will never rise again!

Shearing

'All aboard! All aboard!' is the cry.
  They're a ripping lot of shearers in the shed;
Big Mick, the Speewah ringer, must make skin and trimmings
      fly
  This season if he means to keep ahead;
For Barcoo Ben will run him and half a dozen more
  Of the lank Australian crush upon the board,
And it ain't no use to tell us of the tallies that he shore,
  There'll be records broke this year, you take my word.

'Wool away! Wool away!' is the cry,
  And the merry game of busting is begun!
They're going sheep and sheep, for Big Mick will do or die,
  And the fleecy boys are kept upon the run.
It ain't no kind of joking, it's a game of killing men—
  Up the neck and down the shoulder like a flash,
And the scruffing and the rattle on the battens of the pen
  As to gain a catch the ringer makes a dash.

'Sling 'em out! Sling 'em out!' is the word,
  You can hear the grinding pinions of the press,
Snipping shears and flying brooms upon the board,
  And the sheep are growing wonderfully less.
The shepherds' dogs are barking in the yard,
  And the penner-up is cursing at the back,
And the boss is looking savage at a long Australian card
  With a look that means it's odds he gets the sack.

'Clear the board! Clear the board!' is the shout,
    And Barcoo Ben is caught upon the tail!
Big Mick is smiling grimly as he takes the cobbler out.
    With a lead of two at breakfast he can sail.
The shearers laugh like schoolboys as they hurry from the
    shed,
    There's a clinking of the pannikins and knives,
There's the 'barrack' at the table and the clever things are
    said,
    And yet all those blokes are shearing for their lives.

DAVID McKEE WRIGHT

In the Moonlight

The moon is bright, and the winds are laid, and the river is
    roaring by;
Orion swings, with his belted lights low down in the western
    sky;
North and south from the mountain gorge to the heart of the
    silver plain
There's many an eye will see no sleep till the east grows
    bright again;
There's many a hand will toil to-night, from the centre down
    to the sea;
And I'm far from the men I used to know—and my love is far
    from me.

Where the broad flood eddies the dredge is moored to the
    beach of shingle white,
And the straining cable whips the stream in a spray of silver
    light;

45

The groaning buckets bear their load, and the engine throbs
away,
And the wash pours red on the turning screen that knows not
night or day;
For there's many an ounce of gold to save, from the gorge to
the shining sea—
And there's many a league of the bare brown hills between
my love and me.

Where the lines of gorse are parched and dry, and the sheaves
are small and thin,
The engine beats and the combine sings to the drays that are
leading in,
For they're thrashing out of the stook to-night, and the plain
is as bright as day,
And the fork-tines flash as the sheaves are turned on the frame
of the one-horse dray;
For many a hand will toil to-night, from the mountains down
to the sea;—
But I'm far from the lips of the girl I love, and the heart that
beats for me.

The trappers are out on the hills to-night, and the sickly
lantern-shine
Is mocking the gleam of the silver moon in the scrub on the
long trap-line;
The tallies are big on the rock-strewn spur, and the rattling
clink of the chain
Comes weirdly mixed from the moon-bright hill with the
whistling shriek of pain;
For many a hand will toil to-night where the tussocks are
waving free;—
But it's over the hills and over the plain to the heart that
beats for me.

The stars are bright, and the night is still, and the river is
　　singing by,
And many a face is upward turned to gaze at the moon's
　　bright eye.
North and south, from the forest deeps to the heart of the
　　silver plain,
There's many an eye will see no sleep till the east grows
　　bright again;
There's many a hand will toil to-night by shining land and sea.
O moonlight, bear my message of love to the heart that beats
　　for me.

HUBERT CHURCH

Retrospection

If there were any of the sons of men
Could win from Fate to hold their youth again,
Would any travel more
The paths they trod before?

Would any vex those hyacinthine days
For love of woman, or the many's praise;
The vain delights that trend
To the abhorred end—

Age, that discovers there is nothing worth?
God, when He flung this unessential earth,
Spun it with bias given
To sunder it from Heaven!

HUBERT CHURCH

Favonius

Favonius from the setting sun,
   Sigh, sigh not so upon her tresses!
What though thou diest in the dun,
   She trembled at thy mute caresses.

The rose shall lose her diadem,
   The nightingale shall weep his singing,
And Love shall hear his requiem
   From bells that sorrow sets a-ringing.

Delight is alway in the earth,
   From soul to soul a meteor flying.
And as some spirit gives it birth
   Some other spirit feels it dying.

HUBERT CHURCH

from New Zealand

Ye wandering winds that from your threshing floor,
The immemorial ocean, gather up
Fragrances of the forgotten, if their tears
Weight your vast wings, your indestructible
Motion is girdled with the joy of being
Fresh from the hand of God; and you do take
A path through forests leaning so to hear
Your harmony, until the setting sun

Nets you within his beams; then you do fall
On range and gully, creek and cataract,
And even on the unapportioned strand
Shaken by every billow, as a prayer
Moveth a stubborn heart, and with it sleeps.
What courts are these that ye so vainly urge
For an echoing answer; that are dumb,
Dark oubliettes of foam, and haggard walls
Of terror shaken by the avalanche,
Ever above a desolating fall
Of thunder to a ravine the kea knows,
But nevermore the sun? Oh, surely Time
Here would receive the penitential hours,
As a dear father his returning son!

   .   .   .

  There is a majesty
Of still endurance here; woods recreate
Splendour of mighty shade though tempests reel
Athwart a sail-less hemisphere; the sea
Squanders ablution over the sea wrack
Where dead men lie, and lulls the albatross
Far in her secret South; but never fails
Her due step to these lonely isles and fiords,
Nor ever though the stars and moon be hid
Late cometh to the mountains' inner shrine.

   .   .   .

  There is a dower
Falls from these branches, trembles in the breeze;
And where the light falls variable on a gull
Oaring her snowy breast a power has raised
The splendid motion of the lordless sea
Within our bosom; we are folded in
Harmonious clouds and sunsets, loveliest home

49

Of the serenest thought, the shadowy eaves
Pale of the lucent temple of His glory.
As in a cathedral prayer has made a gloom,
The tribulation of a thousand years
Fallen upon the pillars, here we move
Through cloistered precincts Time has drowsed with
     winds
From the inexorable West. The wave
Tells not the secret of the mocking past;
.The cloud floats lonely from the sea, her heart
Breaks on the mountains; there her song is sung
To alien ears; let the pines draw her down
To weep herself away. We are apart
From this hoar convocation of the hills,
Cataracts, and innumerable groves
Pathed by the bell-bird's anthem, and no more.
Oh! forest listening to eternal years,
And looking to the stars that may have died,
Quenched ere your branches bulbed, if we hear not
The subtle music of the universe
That was before us, and will murmur round
The grave of our last generation wrapped
In ribbed ice, an exhalation falls
From the invisible balm; a spider thread
Of ecstasy floats where our feet have touched
The border-land of Nature's harmony.

HUBERT CHURCH

from A Fugue

There was a music throbbed athwart the street
Few chimes agone. Our charity was wrapped
In a melodious anthem thanking God
We were His chosen—twenty rods away
The music faltered and was heard no more.
Our charity had lived and died therein,
Full as a semibreve, and rich with love
Through a belated bar. The organ shut;
Lights out; and we went home, fast wrapped from cold;
And charity drew not a cuddled hand
From placket to reprieve a soul from death;
Urged on by slow starvation. She will lie,
Through the monotonous, dull minster chime
Till half her gown is swaddled with a wreath
Most pure, most cold—God's silent messengers;
For silence doth forgive and cancel all.

B. E. BAUGHAN

The Ship and the Sea

Day after day, thro' following night on night,
Whether 'twixt Blue and Blue, amid grey calm,
Tempest, or chill disconsolating fog—
Still thro' void air, 'neath one continuing dome
Of mute enormous sky—o'er plain on plain
Of lonely, stark, uninterrupted sea—

From circle to repeated circle of
Mere space for ever changing, aye unchanged:
Voyages on her solitary way
The strong sea-worthy ship.

And she informs that void. The solitude
She peoples, and to all that blank gives point.
Her single presence wakes as to an aim,
Touches, as tho' to sense, the occupants
Of that insensate world. The leashless waves
Race at her side and follow at her heel:
The virgin and clean air dwells in her sails,
And sea-birds, none know whence, sudden appearing,
Hover, as round their mother, at her helm.
The sea is gemm'd with her, the sun's wide eye
Brightens all day on her, and when night comes,
The stars mount up her rigging, the moon slips
White feet upon her sharply-shadow'd decks,
And, in her towers of steady sail high-sitting,
Quietly sings the wind.

More: she herself, this world amid convoys
Another world, and other. Sound of lips
And light of eyes, a burden of warm breath
And hearts toward other hearts that beat, is come
Upon the emptiness—a world of quick,
Doing, devising Consciousness usurps
This kingdom of untroubled oneness—plays
Its sole pulsating part in this huge O
Of unspectator'd theatre . . . and then
As in its entry, in its exit, brief—
Vanishes. The ship passes and is gone.

A rushing star, thro' Heaven's capacious calm
Down-hurling momentary fire: a swift
Passion, that strong on some commanding spirit
Leaps—fastens—fails: or, an importunate fly
That, loud about its little business,
One drowsy second of the summer noon
Awakes, the next falls dead: invading so,
So takes possession, so predominates,
And even so is pass'd the ship, and gone.

She passes. And the indifferent world resumes
Its ancient semblance, and its own device.
Voiceless once more, unpeopled and alone,
One vast monotony magnificent,
The air, the sea, and the infinite sky
Are all—the heart-throbs and the busy minds
Are gone, and wordless comes the wind, the light
No longer sees itself in human eyes,
Nor watch of man is set upon this world.

Nevertheless, it lives, and has its being.
The wind blows on, the sky presides, the sea
Her ageless journeying round the earth pursues,
And onward all the untrodden currents flow.
Man come or gone, 'tis equal. Nature still
Remains, and still the stable elements
Fill their inherent office. Sweet with salt
The free air wanders o'er the wandering waves,
Bright shines the sun upon the shipless sea.

The Old Place

So the last day's come at last, the close of my fifteen year—
The end of the hope, an' the struggles, an' messes I've put in
  here.
All of the shearings over, the final mustering done,—
Eleven hundred an' fifty for the incoming man, near on.
Over five thousand I drove 'em, mob by mob, down the coast;
Eleven-fifty in fifteen year . . . it isn't much of a boast.

Oh, it's a bad old place! Blown out o' your bed half the nights,
And in summer the grass burnt shiny an' bare as your hand,
  on the heights:
The creek dried up by November, and in May a thundering
  roar
That carries down toll o' your stock to salt 'em whole on the
  shore.
Clear'd I have, and I've clear'd an' clear'd, yet everywhere,
  slap in your face,
Briar, tauhinu, an' ruin!—God! it's a brute of a place.
. . . An' the house got burnt which I built, myself, with all
  that worry and pride;
Where the Missus was always homesick, and where she took
  fever, and died.

Yes, well! I'm leaving the place. Apples look red on that
  bough.
I set the slips with my own hand. Well—they're the other
  man's now.
The breezy bluff: an' th clover that smells so over the land,
Drowning the reek o' the rubbish, that plucks the profit out o'
  your hand:

54

That bit o' Bush paddock I fall'd myself, an' watched, each
    year, come clean
(Don't it look fresh in the tawny? A scrap of Old-Country
    green):
This air, all healthy with sun an' salt, an' bright with purity:
An' the glossy karakas there, twinkling to the big blue twink-
    ling sea:
Ay, the broad blue sea beyond, an' the gem-clear cove below,
Where the boat I'll never handle again, sits rocking to and
    fro:
There's the last look to it all! an' now for the last upon
This room, where Hetty was born, an' my Mary died, an'
    John . . .

Well, I'm leaving the poor old place, and it cuts as keen as
    a knife;
The place that's broken my heart—the place where I've lived
    my life.

B. E. BAUGHAN

In Exile

I

The sea is a lonely thing
    Dwelling apart.
Lonely are you and I,
    Heart of my heart.

Lonely the mountain-top
    Stands in the sky.
Sundered as peak and sea
    Are you and I.

The mountain cannot move,
   The sea must stay.
Ruled is the world. We too,
   We must obey.

II

The steady stars of Heaven
   Look down into the brook;
Up from the brook to Heaven
   The stars as steady look.

Amid the vale, the waters
   Undeviating flow.
Past root and rock and forest
   They go as they should go.

What keeps the brook so certain,
   What rhymes the stars so true,
Hath sure some perfect reason
   For parting me and you.

D. H. ROGERS

At Sea

When the southern gale is blowing hard,
The watch are all on the topsail yard.

And when five come down where six went up,
There's one less to share the bite and sup.

A name is missed when the roll they call;
A hand the less for the mainsail haul.

They steal his rags and his bag and bed;
Little it matters to him who's dead.

Instead of the stone and carven verse,
This is his epitaph, curt and terse:
'John Smith, A.B.,
Drowned in latitude 53,
A heavy gale and a following sea.'

We have lost the way to the open sea;
We have missed the doom we hoped to dree.

For the big ships running their easting down
Are far from the din of Sydney town.

Instead of the clean blue sunlit wave,
Our bones will lie in a darksome grave.

For the means to live we barter life.
Would I were back in the old-time strife,
Once more to be
Reefing topsails in 53
In the blinding drift from the angry sea.

D. H. ROGERS

Homeward Bound

They will take us from the moorings, they will tow us down the
    Bay,
    They will pluck us up to wind'ard when we sail.
We shall hear the keen wind whistle, we shall feel the sting of
    spray,

When we've dropped the deep-sea pilot o'er the rail.
Then it's Johnnie heave an' start her, then it's Johnnie roll
and go;
When the mates have picked the watches, there is little rest
for Jack.
But we'll raise the good old chanty that the Homeward-
bounders know,
For the girls have got the tow-rope, an' they're hauling in
the slack.

In the dusty streets and dismal, through the noises of the town,
We can hear the West wind humming through the shrouds;
We can see the lightning leaping when the tropic suns go down,
And the dapple of the shadows of the clouds.
And the salt blood dances in us, to the tune of Homeward
Bound,
To the call to weary watches, to the sheet and to the tack.
When they bid us man the capstan how the hands will walk
her round!—
For the girls have got the tow-rope, an' they're hauling in
the slack.

Through the sunshine of the tropics, round the bleak and
dreary Horn,
Half across the little planet lies our way.
We shall leave the land behind us like a welcome that's outworn
When we see the reeling mastheads swing and sway.
Through the weather fair or stormy, in the calm and in the gale,
We shall heave and haul to help her, we shall hold her on
her track,
And you'll hear the chorus rolling when the hands are making
sail,
For the girls have got the tow-rope, an' they're hauling in
the slack!

WILLIAM STENHOUSE

The Empty Jar

We've lived owre lang, my jar and I,
Far better we were pitten by;
For here I stan', auld and forlorn,
And in my han' a dried-up horn,
While there fornent me looks wi' scorn
      An empty jar.

I hae come thro' a routh o' ill,
But it had never poo'er tae kill
For when my fortunes were depressed
A drap o' whusky made me blest;
But noo, alas! there stands confessed
      An empty jar.

An' were I dowie i' the dumps—
For mortals canna aye haud trumps—
I gat a cronie—ane or twa—
An' roond the jorum we wad ca';
But noo I've only this tae shaw—
      An empty jar.

I ne'er was envious o' the rich,
For happiness is no wi' sich;
But aye I liked an open board,
An' kept ane lang's I could afford;
But noo, alas! my only hoard
      'S an empty jar.

What merry nichts I ca' tae mind
Wi' comrades sociable an' kind,
Wha set the table in a roar
Wi' jest an' story by the score;
But noo the lot o' us deplore
          An empty jar.

Strang drink rank pushon is, some say,
But tae that dictum I say, Nay;
For I hae swilled it frae my youth,
An' fand it unco guid in truth;
An' noo my only fear's, forsooth,
          An empty jar.

I like a man wha's heid is able
Tae stan' his drink an' yet be stable;
But when I meet a sumph sae weak
As no tae ken hoo much tae take,
To him as present I wull make
          An empty jar.

But for mysel' an' twa three mair
I'll ask o' Heaven this simple fare—
Parritch, pease-brose, an' whusky bauld,
Tae fend us frae the bitin' cauld;
And keep frae us when we are auld
          An empty jar.

Sanary

Her little hot room looked over the bay
Through a stiff palisade of glinting palms,
And there she would lie in the heat of the day,
Her dark head resting upon her arms,
So quiet, so still, she did not seem
To think, to feel, or even to dream.

The shimmering, blinding web of sea
Hung from the sky, and the spider sun
With busy frightening cruelty
Crawled over the sky and spun and spun.
She could see it still when she shut her eyes,
And the little boats caught in the web like flies.

Down below at this idle hour
Nobody walked in the dusty street
A scent of dying mimosa flower
Lay on the air, but sweet—too sweet.

KATHERINE MANSFIELD

To L. H. B.

Last night for the first time since you were dead
I walked with you, my brother, in a dream.
We were at home again beside the stream
Fringed with tall berry bushes, white and red.

61

'Don't touch them: they are poisonous,' I said.
But your hand hovered, and I saw a beam
Of strange, bright laughter flying round your head,
And as you stooped I saw the berries gleam.
'Don't you remember? We called them Dead Man's Bread!'
I woke and heard the wind moan and the roar
Of the dark water tumbling on the shore.
Where—where is the path of my dream for my eager feet?
By the remembered stream my brother stands
Waiting for me with berries in his hands . . .
'These are my body. Sister, take and eat.'

R. A. K. MASON

Body of John

Oh I have grown so shrivelled and sere
> *But the body of John enlarges*
> and I can scarcely summon a tear
> *but the body of John discharges*

It's true my old roof is near ready to drop
> *But John's boards have burst asunder*
> and I am perishing cold here atop
> *but his bones lie stark hereunder.*

R. A. K. MASON

After Death

And there will be just as rich fruits to cull
    and jewels to see
    nor shall the moon nor the sun be any more dull
    and there will be flowers as fine to pull
    and the rain will be as beautiful
    but not for me

And there shall be no splendour gone from the vine
    nor from the tree
    and still in the heavens shall glow Jah's radiant sign
    and the dancing sun on horses' sleek hides shall seem no
        less fine
    still shall the car sweep along with as lovely a line
    but not for me

And men shall cut no less curious things upon brass
    still sweep the sea
    nor no little lustrous shadow upon the sand's mass
    cast by the lilting ripple above shall cease to pass
    and radiance still shall enhalo shadows on moonlit grass
    but not for me.

R. A. K. MASON

Sonnet of Brotherhood

Garrisons pent up in a little fort
    with foes who do but wait on every side
    knowing the time soon comes when they shall ride
    triumphant over those rapped and make sport

of them: when those within know very short
is now their hour and no aid can betide:
such men as these not quarrel and divide
but friend and foe are friends in their hard sort

And if these things be so oh men then what
of these beleaguered victims this our race
betrayed alike by Fate's gigantic plot
here in this far-pitched perilous hostile place
this solitary hard-assaulted spot
fixed at the friendless outer edge of space.

R. A. K. MASON

Song of Allegiance

Shakespeare Milton Keats are dead
Donne lies in a lowly bed

Shelley at last calm doth lie
knowing 'whence we are and why'

Byron Wordsworth both are gone
Coleridge Beddoes Tennyson

Housman neither knows nor cares
how 'this heavy world' now fares

Little clinging grains enfold
all the mighty minds of old . . .

They are gone and I am here
　　stoutly bringing up the rear

Where they went with limber ease
　　toil I on with bloody knees

Though my voice is cracked and harsh
　　stoutly in the rear I march

Though my song have none to hear
　　boldly bring I up the rear.

R. A. K. MASON

Be Swift O Sun

Be swift o sun
　　lest she fall on some evil chance:
　　make haste and run
　　to light up the dark fields of France.

See already the moon
　　lies sea-green on our globe's eastern rim:
　　speed to be with her soon:
　　even now her stars grow dim.

Here your labour is null
　　and water poured upon sand
　　to light up the hull
　　which at dawn glimmers on to the land

And here you in vain
    clothe many coming sails with gold
    if you bring not again
    those breasts where I found death of old.

Why bring you ships
    from that evil Dis of a shore
    if you bring not the lips
    I kissed once and shall kiss no more:

O sun make speed
    and delay not to send her your rays
    lest she be in need
    of light in those far alien ways.

That you may single
    my love from the rest, her eyes
    her wide eyes commingle
    all innocence with all things wise:

Raindrops at eve fall
    in your last rays no lovelier:
    her voice is the madrigal
    at your dawn when the first birds stir.

Be swift o sun
    lest she fall on some evil chance:
    make haste and run
    to light up the dark fields of France.

R. A. K. MASON

On the Swag

His body doubled
    under the pack
    that sprawls untidily
    on his old back
    the cold wet deadbeat
    plods up the track

The cook peers out:
    'oh curse that old lag
    here again
    with his clumsy swag
    made of a dirty old
    turnip-bag'

'Bring him in cook
    from the grey level sleet
    put silk on his body
    slippers on his feet,
    give him fire
    and bread and meat

Let the fruit be plucked
    and the cake be iced,
    the bed be snug
    and the wine be spiced
    in the old cove's nightcap:
    for this is Christ.'

R. A. K. MASON

Judas Iscariot

Judas Iscariot
    sat in the upper
    room with the others
    at the last supper

And sitting there smiled
    up at his master
    whom he knew the morrow
    would roll in disaster

At Christ's look he guffawed—
    for then as thereafter
    Judas was greatly
    given to laughter

Indeed they always said
    that he was the veriest
    prince of good fellows
    and the whitest and merriest

All the days of his life
    he lived gay as a cricket
    and would sing like the thrush
    that sings in the thicket.

R. A. K. MASON

Footnote to John ii. 4

Don't throw your arms around me in that way:
    I know that what you tell me is the truth—
    yes I suppose I loved you in my youth
    as boys do love their mothers, so they say,
    but all that's gone from me this many a day:
    I am a merciless cactus an uncouth
    wild goat a jagged old spear the grim tooth
    of a lone crag . . . Woman I cannot stay

Each one of us must do his work of doom
    and I shall do it even in despite
    of her who brought me in pain from her womb,
    whose blood made me, who used to bring the light
    and sit on the bed up in my little room
    and tell me stories and tuck me up at night.

R. A. K. MASON

Ecce Homunculus

Betrayed by friend dragged from the garden hailed
    as prophet and as lord in mockery
    hauled down where Roman Pilate sat on high
    perplexed and querulous, lustily assailed
    by every righteous Hebrew cried down railed
    against by all true zealots . . . still no sigh
    escaped him but he boldly went to die
    made scarcely a moan when his soft flesh was nailed

And so he brazened it out right to the last
    still wore the gallant mask still cried 'divine
    am I, lo for me is heaven overcast'
    though that inscrutable darkness gave no sign
    indifferent or malignant: while he was passed
    by even the worst of men at least sour wine.

R. A. K. MASON

The Young Man Thinks of Sons

Did my father curse his father for his lust I wonder
    as I do mine
    and my grandsire curse his sire for his wickedness his
      weakness his blunder
    and so on down the whole line

Well I'll stop the game break the thread end my race: I will
      not continue
    in the old bad trade:
    I'll take care that for my nerveless mind weakened brain
      neglected sinew
    I alone shall have paid

Let the evil book waste in its swathings the ill pen write not
      one iota
    the ship of doom not sail
    let the sword rot unused in its scabbard let the womb
      lack its quota
    here let my line fail

Let the plough rust untouched of the furrow, yea let the blind
  semen
  stretch vain arms for the virgin:
  I'll hammer no stringed harps for gods to clash discords,
   nor women:
  my orchard won't burgeon

I'll take care that the lust of my loins never bring to fruition
  the seed of a son
  who in his nettle-grown kingdom should curse both my
   sins of commission
  and what I left undone.

R. A. K. MASON

Our Love Was a Grim Citadel

 Our love was a grim citadel:
   no tawdry plaything for the minute
   of strong dark stone we built it well
   and based in the ever-living granite:

 The urgent columns of the years
   press on, like tall rain up the valley:
   and Chaos bids ten thousand spears
   run to erase our straw-built folly.

71

R. A. K. MASON

Prelude

This short straight sword
    I got in Rome
    when Gaul's new lord
    came tramping home:

It did that grim
    old rake to a T . . .
    if it did him,
    well, it does me

Leave the thing of pearls
    with silken tassels
    to priests and girls
    and currish vassals

Here's no fine cluster
    on the hilt this drab
    blade lacks lustre—
    but it can stab.

D. M. ROSS

Bloody Bill

Ho! are you there, Bill Hawkins,
Below the cruising shark,
Down with the ribbon frost-fish
In dungeons of green dark?

Old Bloody Bill, you rover,
  Where is your Devil school
Combed from foul dens and brothels
  By crimps of Liverpool?

Here over Port Moeraki
  The heavens still are blue;
An amethystine ocean
  Runs north to Oamaru.

Oh, many times and hoarsely
  You damned the leadsman's soul
Who told the ebbing fathoms
  On the uncharted shoal;

And twice in midnight smother
  From keelson unto truck
You felt the mounting shiver
  When the brave whaler struck.

Now to old Port Moeraki
  No more the captains come
Salt as the junk they fed on,
  Cured in Jamaica rum.

Remember how, carousing,
  Into the pail of gin
Between loud oaths and laughter
  We dipped the pannikin?

Though red of eye and drunken
  The hogs went to their swill,
One ever looking seaward
  Kept watch on Flagstaff Hill.

73

And drunk or sober, Hawkins,
  You bent men to the oar,
For there was naught to hinder
  Of law beyond the shore.

The try-pots now are rusted—
  Rusted and overturned—
And dark and damp the charcoal
  Lies where the red fire burned.

The grand old fleet has vanished,
  All save some rotting bones,
Along the coasts that harbor
  The keels of Johnnie Jones;

Where Abel Jansen Tasman
  His frightened northway took,
Where gleaming Nick's Head beaconed
  The bay for Captain Cook.

Flaunting your God-defiance,
  All merciless you sailed
To harry and to plunder
  Wherever wrong prevailed.

God knows how you went scatheless
  Past pirates of Malay
To cram your hold with blackbirds
  Down Raratonga way!

You lie down there, Bill Hawkins,
  With red blood on each hand,
Nor can the currents clean them
  Nor can the drifting sand.

And yet with you, old sailor,
　What paltry feud have I?
You chose the rover's living,
　His bold, brave way to die.

To make a future Eden
　The killers first must come
To tame unfriended peoples
　With lust and lash and rum.

And Christ must follow after
　And walk the water-way
When want has stung the heathen
　Or greed has made him pray.

Here now your son, Bill Hawkins,
　Makes rioting his sport;
Your daughter leads the *haka*,
　The lithest moll in port.

And yonder one-eyed Susan
　Has all the coast in view
From Blueskin Bay, far southward,
　Right north past Oamaru.

She sleeps; and, damned or salvaged,
　Best fitted to God's will,
You called the tune, Bill Hawkins,
　And paid for Bloody Bill.

D'ARCY CRESSWELL

The Impatient Poet

Love, men's honour, many ripening deeds,
The level happiness of measured needs,
From these the impatient poet turns aside
To see Apollo singing in his stride
From dawn till dusk. Once seen, how less it were
What men are kings, what women coil their hair!

D'ARCY CRESSWELL

To L——

If ever I suspect thee of a lie,
Condemn it not so long as thou art true;
Love uses doubt to prove perfection by,
And lives on proof, where nothing less will do.
This being so, most often love doth die
For want of proof to prove so deep a thing;
Men's doubts grow deeper as they search the sky
They can its bounds within their compass bring.
Whenever thy affections thus I prove,
And find them, like the heavens, fix'd and fair,
Too soon the ever-mounting lark, my love,
Finds him outstripp'd and fancies nothing there.
Then like a heavy stone he doth descend,
Ah, heavy doubt! to doubt his dearest friend.

D'ARCY CRESSWELL

Time Lags Abed

I notic'd how the spent and speechless year
Not suddenly was gone, but leaf by leaf
Surrender'd her dominion to the sheaf,
And looking back, did slowly disappear.
Nor hungry winter at a bound was near:
Bright days delay'd him for a season brief;
Nor spring comes all in view, but like a thief
Picks with each sweet his locks, and lo! is here.
Time lags abed with change: the engendering hour
Breeds on its opposite: so by the night
The pregnant moon's delivered of her light;
So on most hazard men hatch deeds of power;
So are sweet sonnets got from grievings sour;
So shall my day that's doubtful yet be bright.

D'ARCY CRESSWELL

from Lyttelton Harbour

VIII

Home did I say, ye homeless? Not to ye.
Ye are the shadow on this lovely show,
A moment's darkness on a moonlit sea,
A mire of aimless cattle on bright snow.
Not to your vain appearance do I go,
But here the world of Nature now to me
Unlocks its lonely entrance, and I know
The light within which you shall never see

Except you learn to follow. 'Twas for this
I fell among you and believ'd your laws:
That her eternal law more honour'd is
In my contrition. Now on these wild shores,
By these withstanding hills, the instant bliss
Springs in my heart, more welcome for that pause.

XXXIII

Thou bent and only motion of our lives,
Thou clear propensity of perfect hearts,
From shore to shore the blissful zephyr drives
Our striving sails—one vessel of all arts
And powers that for the main of Time departs
But makes no harbour, and Mankind deprives
Of shelter more; and each light skiff that darts
The narrow strait and makes the port it strives.
Greece, thou art gone; and Time's white billow knows
Where thou art hid. And now my spirit sees
The crack'd and founder'd navy of thy foes
All helmless drift on shores how like to these!
The level, dark, as breathing of new woes;
The strand, how bright, with what strange wealth of trees!

XXXVIII

Ye barren hearts and bitter, steep'd in brine;
Ye empty lives where nothing native grows
In that bare world ye worship! Here in mine
Proudly within her covert climbs the rose,
Where in the dark the horrid satyr goes
To dabble in the brook that feeds the vine,
And hide him when the morning-breeze half-shows
The watching Pleiades within the pine.

Then Phoebus' coming the complexion'd cloud
Shall turn to silver; and the merry Pan
Awake the Muses in their mountain shroud;
And all the sensual growths to music fan;
And on the rock the cricket cry aloud
Like morning singing in the heart of Man.

MARY URSULA BETHELL

Pause

When I am very earnestly digging
I lift my head sometimes, and look at the mountains,
And muse upon them, muscles relaxing.

I think how freely the wild grasses flower there,
How grandly the storm-shaped trees are massed in their
  gorges
And the rain-worn rocks strewn in magnificent heaps.

Pioneer plants on those uplands find their own footing;
No vigorous growth, there, is an evil weed:
All weathers are salutary.

It is only a little while since this hillside
Lay untrammelled likewise,
Unceasingly swept by transmarine winds.

In a very little while, it may be,
When our impulsive limbs and our superior skulls
Have to the soil restored several ounces of fertiliser,

The Mother of all will take charge again,
And soon wipe away with her elements
Our small fond human enclosures.

Detail

My garage is a structure of excessive plainness,
It springs from a dry bank in the back garden,
It is made of corrugated iron,
And painted all over with brick-red.

But beside it I have planted a green Bay-tree,
—A sweet Bay, an Olive, and a Turkey Fig,
—A Fig, an Olive, and a Bay.

MARY URSULA BETHELL

Weather

More rain has fallen this winter
Than in the winters of twenty-one years past.
The oldest inhabitant does not remember
A winter of so many violent storms.
Soil water-logged. Season retarded. Gardens undone.
    (The ever-dismal daily paper!)

But orange Poor Man, who did sulk for nine months,
And threw off all his leaves, and shivered naked,
Is covering his twigs with little bright green knobs.
Montana Rubens, wept for dead not long since,
Has turned herself into a delightful garland.

MARY URSULA BETHELL

The Long Harbour

There are three valleys where the warm sun lingers,
gathered to a green hill girt-about anchorage,
and gently, gently, at the cobbled margin
of fire-formed, time-smoothed, ocean-moulded curvature,
a spent tide fingers the graven boulders,
the black, sea-bevelled stones.

The fugitive hours, in those sun-loved valleys,
implacable hours, their golden-wheeled chariots'
inaudible passage check, and slacken
their restless teams' perpetual galloping;
and browsing, peaceable sheep and cattle
gaze as they pause by the way.

Grass springs sweet where once thick forest
gripped vales by fire and axe freed to pasturage;
but flame and blade have spared the folding gullies,
and there, still, the shade-flitting, honey-sipping lutanists
copy the dropping of tree-cool waters
dripping from stone to stone.

White hawthorn hedge from old, remembered England,
and orchard white, and whiter bridal clematis
the bush-bequeathed, conspire to strew the valleys
in tender spring, and blackbird, happy colonist,
and blacker, sweeter-fluted tui echo
either the other's song.

From far, palm-feathery, ocean-spattered islands
there rowed hither dark and daring voyagers;
and Norseman, Gaul, the Briton and the German
sailed hither singing; all these hardy venturers
they desired a home, and have taken their rest there,
and their songs are lost on the wind.

I have walked here with my love in the early spring-time,
and under the summer-dark walnut-avenues,
and played with the children, and waited with the aged
by the quayside, and listened alone where manukas
sighing, windswept, and sea-answering pine-groves
garrison the burial-ground.

It should be very easy to lie down and sleep there
in that sequestered hillside ossuary,
underneath a billowy, sun-caressed grass-knoll,
beside those dauntless, tempest-braving ancestresses
who pillowed there so gladly, gnarled hands folded,
their tired, afore-translated bones.

It would not be a hard thing to wake up one morning
to the sound of bird-song in scarce-stirring willow-trees,
waves lapping, oars plashing, chains running slowly,
and faint voices calling across the harbour;
to embark at dawn, following the old forefathers,
to put forth at daybreak for some lovelier,
still undiscovered shore.

MARY URSULA BETHELL

Spring Snow and Tui

We said: there will surely be hawthorn out
down in the sun-holding folds of the hills by the sea;
but suddenly snow had forestalled the thorns there,
death-white and cold on their boughs hung the festival
    wreaths.

It is all one. The same hand scatters the blossoms
of winter and spring-time. The black-robed psalmodist,
traversing swiftly the silent landscape like Azrael,
echoed in clear repetition his well-tuned antiphon;
a waking bugle it might be, a passing bell,
of life, death, life, life telling: it is all one.

MARY URSULA BETHELL

Looking Down on Mesopotamia

    Not as in time past, mountainy spaces,
    not as in time past, great solitudes,
    no more can you, deep silences,
    speak the consoling word.

    Again at sundown I have watched the tussock
    glow and fade to pallor, merge with darkness
    where rain-hewn rocks, ice-chiselled bastions
    bleed to death in cataracts of stones.

Down on the valley floor how lovely
now the thin strands of Rangitata river,
on leaden ground their silver damascene,
too deep below to discover sound or motion,
all still and set the sinuous pattern shows.

High above riverbed now veers a questing seagull,
so far, so small, so sharply white and black, he takes
my gaze. Moving he moves not, yet is moving,
advanced to his intention and his end.

Night falls. The uttermost crests
burn to the sun's good-bye. . . .
It is the hour of sacrifice. Those fires
are sacrificial. . . . As to the wind his pinion
gives ocean-homing seagull, repose and impulse one,
so to the high places we bring earth's burden,
the travail, stress, and patience of the ages,
so to the high altars the heart's anguish,
our grief, our desolation, even our despair. . . .

Night has fallen. Earth sleeps wrapped round
with the sure purpose of eternity.

EILEEN DUGGAN

Pilgrimage

Now are the bells unlimbered from their spires
In every steeple-loft from pole to pole.
The four winds wheel and blow in to this gate,
And every wind is wet with carillons.

84

The two Americas at eagle-height,
The pure, abstracted Himalayan chimes.
Great ghosts of clappers from the Russian fries
And sweet wind-sextoned tremblers from Cathay;
The bells of Ireland jesting all the way,
The English bells, slow-bosomed as a swan,
The queenly, weary din of Notre Dame,
And the Low Countries ringing back the sea;
Then Spain, the Moor still moaning through the saint,
The firry, frosty bells of Germany,
And on before them, baying, sweeping down,
The heavy, joyful pack of thunderjowls
That tongue hosannas from the leash of Rome—
All float untethered over Jaffa Gate,
To fling one peal, when angels cheat the stone.
But if one little gaping country bell,
Blown from its weather-boarding in the south,
Should be too lost to keep its covenant
Or lift its heart and reins up to the hour,
Know that its dumbness riots more than sound.

EILEEN DUGGAN

Interlude

It was the wildest vanity
I thought that bird began for me.

And just as I, who fail and fail,
Thought I had passed the blackbird's pale,

It was recalled to me afresh
Pride is conceived with mortal flesh,

For he broke off, forgetting all,
And sang four pure, plain notes, a call

That startled him as well as me.
It was such aimless ecstasy,

Unwary even in a bird,
A joy too naked to be heard!

Once on a sun-rinsed country day,
A barefoot boy, called in from play,

Came on an errand to our door,
And, at a loss upon the floor,

Knuckled one toe against the next,
Forgot the message, verse and text,

Broke off as if in some surprise
And smiled and smiled into my eyes.

What thought had sent that joyous stress,
That same defenceless happiness?

This is the only power of dust,
Its miracle, not flesh, but trust—

It passes water, flame, and air,
That have less reason for despair,

By this great, absent faith in joy
That comes unsought to bird and boy.

EILEEN DUGGAN

The Tides Run Up the Wairau

The tides run up the Wairau
That fights against their flow.
My heart and it together
Are running salt and snow.

For though I cannot love you,
Yet, heavy, deep, and far,
Your tide of love comes swinging,
Too swift for me to bar.

Some thought of you must linger,
A salt of pain in me,
For oh what running river
Can stand against the sea?

EILEEN DUGGAN

The Bushfeller

Lord, mind your trees to-day!
My man is out there clearing.
God send the chips fly safe.
My heart is always fearing.

And let the axehead hold!
My dreams are all of felling.
He earns our bread far back.
And then there is no telling.

If he came home at nights,
We'd know, but it is only—
We might not even hear—
A man could lie there lonely.

God, let the trunks fall clear,
He did not choose his calling;
He's young and full of life—
A tree is heavy, falling.

EILEEN DUGGAN

Post-War

The worst burn is to come
Though countries blaze like bush,
One moment running song,
The next a blackened hush.

What though the bush-fire's flames
Whirl like a high sunspot,
By paddock suckling seed,
Its roar is soon forgot.

But not so soon by all
For fear is deeper bound.
Though loam may cease to catch,
Peat burns underground.

EILEEN DUGGAN

Victory

It comes to this, in plain words,
You will be defeated
By those who have no arms
And have not even retreated.

Back to original night
You will drive each defenceless city,
But in the eyes underground
There will be only pity.

Though, in contempt of life,
You slew the last defying,
Into your very ranks
His spirit would come flying.

When the learned have all despaired
For liberty departed,
This planet will be saved
By the simple-hearted.

More even, the universe,
Since space and time are shrinking!
What our star takes to heart
Its kind may yet be thinking.

The gentle are used to destroy
But the ultimate peace shall hinge
By an awful equity
On their unsought revenge.

It may even be
That under their frozen woe,
Bearing and bearing down,
You will snap like boughs in snow.

The humble shall sentence in kind
Those who winter the world by law.
Some may not be slain but live,
Forgotten in the thaw.

EILEEN DUGGAN

Contrast

It was so cold the skyline seemed to splinter
As the ice in the puddles cracked beneath the camels.
The great statute that we know as winter,
Unsoftened yet by any Spring amendment,
Was full enforced—a sumptuary law,
Forbidding earth undue indulgence
In leaf and flower, in hip and haw.

The caravan swayed like a ship under canvas when its topsails
    belly in the wind,
And the Magi looked over the rolling dunes
As a sailor to shore in his mind.
Their light in the dusk was like a lantern at a mast-head,
Seen dipping, the bluer for the salt air, afar off;
And their thought was deep and slow and undulating
Like the rising and falling of a galley in the sea's trough—
All very leisurely as demand great distances—
And the star, as slow as reason, undulated too.

Ah but the shepherds on the hill above the grotto,
Like a bolt from the blue,
Hurtled headlong, helter-skelter, wild-foot, down the
  cragside,
As fast as instinct—no conjecture, no dismay!
They had not watched for years; they had not calculated;
But they knew the way.

J. C. BEAGLEHOLE

from Considerations on Certain Music of J. S. Bach

I

Meditating in silence after the last note
I consider old John Sebastian
cantor and capellmeister, official writer
of Leipzig anthems, player in court bands,
chief of the sons of God, by his music divine
in his own right beyond the Lutheran God.
He was twice married, had eighteen children . . . he was
twice married, had eighteen children; mark that
my soul: the genius philoprogenitive,
historical instance for once; was, too,
a model of conjugal stability; prayed
piously; quarrelled with his churchwardens;
taught Latin. Colossal!—and lived to sixty-five,
producing and teaching all those small Bachs—
must have lost count of children and anthems alike!
Regularity did it; punctual
to the Sunday Bach with his anthems; punctual
I suppose with his offspring: man must work,
his days are numbered, the old cantor must produce.

And his works were good—his Wilhelm Friedemann,
young Johann Christian and the rest, good musicians,
and his anthems that outlasted them all.
So I consider in front of the clavier
old John Sebastian tempered so well,
playing his forty-eight preludes and fugues, sublime
manifesto: more final than that later one
of communist Marx. The fugue that I played—
it closed on a cadence like the hours of his life,
when the old man lay dictating that last
choral-prelude, last elaboration of faith
and dying humbleness before his God.
Wenn wir in höchsten Nöthen sein—troubled those words
but how transfigured, in trust glorified.
And yet consider that annoyed fierce cantor's face
of his portrait, the just indignation
of a virtuous man affronted with a false note,
with a choir attacking at a wrong angle
some *Sanctus* or *Kyrie*; John Sebastian,
master, I much prefer your Forty-eight;
your face for the excellent Leipzig musicians—
out of strength sweetness: give me the honey! . . .
That prelude flowed like a spring of consolation
in a hard southern land; come, my fingers,
over the page, forget the multiplied children,
that severe Leipzig physiognomy,
court bands, conjugal stability and Latin;
to it again—to the tenderness, sad
beauty, to the firm exquisite line, the lovely
pulsation and triumph of order: turn,
this next is John Sebastian himself, cantor,
his soul and mind; then to our fifth French Suite.

A. R. D. FAIRBURN

Winter Night

The candles gutter and burn out,
  and warm and snug we take our ease,
and faintly comes the wind's great shout
  as he assails the frozen trees.

The vague walls of this little room
  contract and close upon the soul;
deep silence hangs amid the gloom;
  no sound but the small voice of the coal.

Here in this sheltered firelit place
  we know not wind nor shivering tree;
we two alone inhabit space,
  locked in our small infinity.

This is our world, where love enfolds
  all images of joy, all strife
resolves in peace: this moment holds
  within its span the sum of life.

For Time's a ghost: these reddening coals
  were forest once ere he'd begun,
and now from dark and timeless boles
  we take the harvest of the sun;

and still the flower-lit solitudes
  are radiant with the springs he stole
where violets in those buried woods
  wake little blue flames in the coal.

Great stars may shine above this thatch;
   beyond these walls perchance are men
with laws and dreams: but our thin latch
   holds all such things beyond our ken.

The fire that lights our cloudy walls
   now fails beneath the singing pot,
and as the last flame leaps and falls
   the far wall is and then is not.

Now lovelier than firelight is the gleam
   of dying embers, and your face
shines through the pathways of my dream
   like young leaves in a forest place.

A. R. D. FAIRBURN

Landscape with Figures

(Memories of England, 1930)

No dragon's blood breaking in crimson flowers,
   no timeless jungle, obscenity of apes,
no serpents lust-entangled in hot bowers
   where in the moonlight flit the tiger-shapes;

no crunch of living bones, no clouds that rise
   malarial from the whining swamp where falls
death in a raindrop from the envenomed skies,
   no jackal's wail beneath the desert walls—

but only meadowlarks, armorial shields,
   and woods of wishing-green with buds bedight,
and vicars tripping home through daisied fields,
   and mezzotints, and dairymaid's delight.

Behold the springtime and the freshening east!
  Now fabulous in leaves the adder dwells
to bite the hand, sole spice to all this feast
  of harmless primrose, heaven-coloured bells.

Blue blood's behind sad walls where birds are bred
  and no more kings. By dim baronial scenes
along arterial roads runs common red,
  and pulses down green lanes in limousines.

Fur-coated abstinence and gilt-edged stock
  strew petrol mists where flit the hiker-shapes,
and charabancs go lumbering choc-a-bloc
  with rougy jades and sleek unjungled apes.

No panther-lust, nor hunger for hot flesh
  mars England's rectories! Here matrons coy
and dutiful divines their souls refresh
  with love-in-jaegers, simple beefsteak joy.

From this cold earth Crusaders leapt in fire
  to barbarous lands, and roving knights in ships
in death's despite set forth to swage desire,
  with Christ a lovely flame upon their lips.

In mortgaged precincts epicene Sir Giles,
  cold remnant of a fiery race, consorts
with pale fox-hunting Jews with glossy smiles,
  and plays at Walton Heath, and drives a sports.

One Race, One Flag

Smith
a refugee from the Black Country
suffers the insults of the foreman
that his family may live
in the discomfort to which they are accustomed
with deductions by the Commissioner of Taxes.
Smith has four sons,
hands-in-pockets, fronting chaos;
limbs of a ring-barked tree, losing sap.
Smith is an English immigrant.
Consider the curious fate
of the English immigrant:
his wages were taken from him
and exported to the colonies;
sated with abstinence, gorged on deprivation,
he followed them: to be confronted on arrival
with the ghost of his back wages, a load of debt;
the bond of kinship, the heritage of Empire.

A. R. D. FAIRBURN

Song

(*from To Daphnis and Chloe in the Park*)

O lovers, this song I give to you,
the words are old and bitter and true:
east or west, north or south,
trust no ear and trust no mouth

put no trust in earth or sky
stare at the world with a brassy eye
lie dissemble and evade
seek out your reckless glade
O let your lips be warm
flesh sing before the storm
maid and man
take what you can
before the heart grows cold
the mind desperate and the body old.

A. R. D. FAIRBURN

La Belle Dame sans Merci

Discarding even the bag of chocolates and the novel
I climbed into that hovel
on wheels the second-class smoker
praying that Fate the irrepressible joker
would grant me release
permit me the hypnotic peace
of wheels clicking on rails for a few
beautiful hours but by God who
should be there who by God's grace
but the fat spent woman with a face
bitter as a holy war
she whom so often before
I had met in my stifling crayfish dreams
(waking with screams)
and with her the grim
wolf-jaw (husband escort paramour or fifth limb)

97

with the orange-and-chocolate blazer
and the smart-alec shoes.
Her voice was like a razor
at the throat of quiet. She was slanging
the foes of Justice. The trouble was there hadn't been a
   hanging
and when it came to murder she was no latitudinarian
and definitely not a vegetarian
the faintest stink of blood
made her feel good
and even her mental picture of the gallows' action
appeared to give her some (strictly biological) satisfaction
but a spoil-sport Cabinet had stepped in and stopped the fun
just when it really had begun.
Doncher reckon they oughter put him on the end of a string
the murdering bastard doncher reckon and let him swing
I'd like to do the job
with me own hands the slob
and by God if they'd let me so I would
I'd fix his lordship I'd fix him good
and proper and let him rot
but they haven't got
the guts to slip a noose
round his dirty ears
hell in twenty years
he'll be running around again loose
and none of us
safe at night he'll have the run of us
just because of a few
fools in Wellington . . .
                    And you
you don't believe in religion do you? wheeling
on me with acid relevance and I feeling

I was in some sense conniving at a threat
to this poor woman's life and honour I couldn't get
a word out of my mouth and felt very much to blame
and overcome with shame.
Oh Mr Tennyson, your dream of fair women,
how it echoes remotely, at this late date, a lemon!

A. R. D. FAIRBURN

Night Song

Though Time's black mountain overhangs
    the night where she's engrossed in sleep
its shadow cannot bruise my love,
    so calm she lies, she dreams so deep.

She is not hurt by what shall be,
    death stands enchanted in her eyes;
remote and lovely, a floating flower
    on the lily pool of sleep she lies.

Dream deep, my love, as in the time
    when your sweet spirit was unborn,
but rise up when the east is purple
    and dress your hair for Judgment morn.

A. R. D. FAIRBURN

Full Fathom Five

He was such a curious lover of shells
and the hallucinations of water
that he could never return out of the sea
without first having to settle a mermaid's bill.

Groping along the sea-bottom of the age
he discovered many particulars he did not care to speak about
even in the company of water-diviners
things sad and unspeakable
moss-covered skulls with bodies fluttering inside
with the unreality of specks moving before the eyes of a
    photograph
trumpets tossed from the decks of ocean-going liners
eccentric starfish fallen from impossible heavens
fretting on uncharted rocks
still continents with trees and houses like a child's drawing
and in every cupboard of the ocean
weary dolphins trapped in honey-coloured cobwebs
murmuring to the revolution Will you be long.

He was happy down there under the frothing ship-lanes
because nobody ever bothered him with statistics
or talk of yet another dimension of the mind.

And eventually and tragically finding he could not drown
he submitted himself to the judgment of the desert
and was devoured by man-eating ants
with a rainbow of silence branching from his lips.

A. R. D. FAIRBURN

A Farewell

What is there left to be said?
There is nothing we can say,
nothing at all to be done
to undo the time of day;
no words to make the sun
roll east, or raise the dead.

I loved you as I love life:
the hand I stretched out to you
returning like Noah's dove
brought a new earth to view,
till I was quick with love;
but Time sharpens his knife,

Time smiles and whets his knife,
and something has got to come out
quickly, and be buried deep,
not spoken or thought about
or remembered even in sleep.
You must live, get on with your life.

A. R. D. FAIRBURN

from Disquisition on Death

I

I went through the market-place crying, There is no death,
and was greeted only by the frightened laughter of fools
who live in such terror of the dissolution
and decay of their pitiful bodies that they see
only the faggots, and not the fire of God.
Take comfort, little ones, I said. How should Homunculus
flare on the void, how should he cause a disruption
of the elements? That Leonardo at his going-out
was attended with lightning is well within our credence,
but surely death for the poor in spirit is only
a matter of degree, bringing no great change in their estate?
Yet it may be that their fear of the dark is well-founded,
for they are temporal stuff, rooted in earth,
reared on unleavened bread, and well may they find
the wine of immortality strange tipple.

II

It is this body-death they fear indeed,
this scavenger of flesh and all living substance,
this is the very fountainhead of fear.
How should so beautiful a thing as death
be a stench in the nostrils, be clothed in such bitter finality?
For death is but the digestive organ of God,
by its prime metabolism giving
fresh form and shape to the immortal spirit;
so that the leaf, the fruit, bowel and gut of swine,
the beggar's scabs, the flesh of emperors,

the lips of Guinivere and the blood of Christ,
dissolved and scattered, have worn a million shapes.
We are one flesh, one spirit, and all that is
shines fair in the eyes of God. Nothing so low
but is a part of us, of our true being,
and we love all, so we be pure in heart.
But some there be who defile God's living word,
saints and ascetics who sunder flesh from soul,
hoping in woeful ambition to raise man's spirit
to a higher dignity. They gaze on God's handiwork
and say, It is not good. They make of the flesh
a beastly and ungodly thing. So by their vile deceit
and betrayal of God's gracious trust have they brought
the spirit low and made it one in kind
with their blasphemous illusion.
But let us rather follow our father Rabelais,
who by the alchemy of a bright and loving mind
would raise all beastly things to the brink of godhead.

III

Kant's dead, the gods be praised.
That old man ruled me five years or more,
wagging the finger of reproof under my nose,
bloodless, lifeless, sexless he ruled me,
he and his system, a two-and-elevenpenny clock
with an alarm like the conscience of Calvin.
He's dead, and I no more eat German haggis.
I came upon him in a corner of the park
and pushed my umbrella through his newspaper,
so that he died old with no dazzling of eyes.
Let him rot slowly.
Let his end be modest and seemly, no whit spectacular.
A decent, quiet end, if you please, Master Death.

A. R. D. FAIRBURN

Epithalamium

We have found our peace, and move with the turning globe;
the night is all about us, the lovers' robe.

Mortal my love, my strength: your beauty their wound.
Strip quickly darling, your fingers be the wind

undressing a snowy peak to the sun's love,
scatter your clouds, be Everest, O my Eve.

Leap on the bed, lie still, your body truth become dream
torturing my arms before their kingdom come.

Give the wise their negations, the moralists their maps;
our empire the moment, the geometer's point where all shapes

of delight are hidden as joy sleeps in the vine.
I tell you again, what the poor have always known,

that this is all the heaven we shall ever find
in all our footsore and fatal journey and beyond,

and we shall never have enough to keep out foul weather,
or to eke out age, will perish forgetful of each other,

yet breeding saints or subduing Asia set against this
were violating our lives with littleness.

Now at the brink of being, in our pride of blood
let us remember lost lovers, think of the dead

who have no power, who aching in earth lie,
the million bones, white longings in the night of eternity.

O love, how many of our faith have fallen!
Endless the torrent of time, endless and swollen

with tributaries from the broken veins of lovers.
I kiss you in remembrance of all true believers.

Midnight thoughts. Dark garlands to adorn your flesh
so it shine like snow, like fire. Flakes of ash

blowing from doom's far hill. Such wisps of terror
gazed at too long even in your body's mirror

would disrupt our continent, drain our seas,
bring all to nothing. Love, let us laugh and kiss,

only your lips but not with speech can tell
moving in the darkness what is unspeakable,

and though your eyes reflect spring's green and yellow like a
pool
I cannot see them, can only guess at what is more beautiful

than home at last, than a child's sleep, more full of pity
and gentleness than snow falling on a burning city.

A. R. D. FAIRBURN

The Impetuous Lover

This is the time, the appointed place,
   love's paratroops have hit the ground,
surprise is scrawled across your face—
   soft, not a sound!

The floor sways up to meet the wall,
   my blood is up, my cab can't wait.
Tell me, before the pictures fall,
   tell me my fate!

Tell me with passion's flaming tongue
   as here before your throne I kneel,
tell me, before the trap is sprung—
   how do you feel?

Speak to me now, for love's sweet sake,
   send me a wire, my gay entrancer.
I warn you I shall never take
   'NO!' for an answer.

See—in my buttonhole I wear
   the tiger lily of desire!
Its fumes are more than flesh can bear—
   SPEAK, OR I FIRE!

A. R. D. FAIRBURN

Song at Summer's End

Down in the park the children play
rag-happy through the summer day
with dirty feet and freckled faces,
laughing, fighting, running races.
Dull against the smoky skies
the summer's heavy burden lies,
leaden leaves on tired trees
lacking supple limbs like these.

The skyline shows the shape of life,
tomorrow's world of sweat and strife,
fifty stacks and one grey steeple.
Down the street come factory people,
folk who used to play on swings,
dodging chores and apron-strings
to wrestle on the grass and run
barefoot with the fleeting sun.

Some of the kids are sailing boats;
the first leaf drops unheeded, floats
and dances on the muddy pond.
Shadows from the world beyond
lengthen, sprawl across the park;
day rolls onward towards the dark.
From the clock-tower, wreathed in smoke,
Time speaks gravely, stroke on stroke.

A. R. D. FAIRBURN

Beggar to Burgher

I am a man defeated in his loins:
  custom and law have hit me where I live.
Look me over. Laugh at me. Toss no coins.
  I'm asking nothing, sir, that's yours to give.

You have no news to tell me, bad or good.
  I know it all, what soul or body lacks.
I sweat, and sleep, and starve—or chop your wood
  for tucker. When I go mad I fire your stacks.

Sir, here we are, the two of us, rich and poor,
  I in my winter doss, or summer ditch,
you in your linen, comfortable, secure.
  One of us should be envious—tell me which?

I am a man confounded. Yet my defeat
  is something short of absolute. O bold
hunter, O proud proprietor, I repeat—
  I'm asking nothing, sir, that's yours to withhold.

Exhibit her proudly, the trophy of your chase,
  like a horned head (true symbol of your power!),
but know that your corn-stack was our lying-place,
  learn that the man of straw has had his hour.

A. R. D. FAIRBURN

from To a Friend in the Wilderness

Old friend, dear friend,
your voice comes to me through the scrawled words
like a bell ringing in the riotous midnight,
like news of peace through static.
                     I hear the leaves
rustle above your door. On the sun-baked path
the cat lies dreaming. Noon-tranced, the pig
sleeps in the shade. Your house stands,
a cavernous rock in a sea of light. In the passage
a wisp of breeze or a poltergeist stirs the cobweb.
The sun is exalted, climbs
to his throne of noon. In the crystal heat the cicadas
crackle on sunlit walls, on pea-sticks dried and splintered,
and among the macrocarpas:
from thistle to cloudless blue the world is vibrant.
Even the inner rooms are pervaded with noon,
the whole world a hot room hung with green leaves.

Beyond the pampas bushes
the sea snores on the shingle, boils lazily among the rocks.
There lie the umber weeds, combings
from the sea's hair, there sparkle
salt crystals on the pearl and amber shells.
No need to tell me of these things, no need
for letters. I am with you, and we sit again
on the old log half-buried in the sand,
sucking our pipes, happy to talk of things
we shall never understand, our smoke wreathing

on the still air in the pattern of our thoughts,
eyes narrowed in the glare
of sun and sea to watch the falling wave
that holds the summer in its green concave.

A. R. D. FAIRBURN

Down on My Luck

Wandering above a sea of glass
   in the soft April weather,
wandering through the yellow grass
   where the sheep stand and blether;
roaming the cliffs in the morning light,
   hearing the gulls that cry there,
not knowing where I'll sleep tonight,
   not much caring either.

I haven't got a stiver,
   the tractor's pinched my job
I owe the bar a fiver
   And the barman fifteen bob;
the good times are over,
   the monkey-man has foreclosed,
the woman has gone with the drover,
   not being what I supposed.

I used to set things spinning,
   I used to dress like a lord,
mostly I came out winning,
   but all that's gone by the board;

my pants have lost their creases,
    I've fallen down on my luck,
the world has dropped to pieces,
    everything's come unstuck.

Roaming the cliffs in the morning light,
    hearing the gulls that cry there,
not knowing where I'll sleep tonight,
    not much caring, either,
wandering above a sea of glass
    in the soft April weather,
wandering through the yellow grass
    close to the end of my tether.

ROBIN HYDE

The English Rider

That girl who always wore the Harris tweeds
Riding to hounds—I don't recall her name—
Tweeds, and a sulky mouth; but all the same,
In some vague manner, she seemed typical
Of all this little country thinks it needs.
No gorse in her, I mean, no smouldering flame,
Brought up from kiddie days to play the game,
Any damned game, archery, basketball;
I don't believe the frosty kisses pall
On English mouths. Not unattractive, no—
A hint of blood-red berries in the snow,
That quite unspeakable self-confidence
Of silk-worms not cut down on mulberry leaves,
Just the right stockings. But she'd take a fence
Calm as a desperate man. One half believes

Something cried out in her, 'Christ, let me fall!—
Let the hare off, this once.' Well, there's your trick
Britishers play, against the stale cards stacked
By the world's cardsharps. Just that silvery quick
Jingle of stirrups, a young fool, unbacked
Except by youth, riding past hazards. Yes,
She looked as if she rode to fall. I guess
Her seat was good, she wouldn't stop to think
About the red tongue, lolling, mad to drink,
The hunted in the thorn-brakes. But she'd ride
With the taut English look of deep-cut pride.
You'd think, 'She's just a kid, not come to bloom—
A jonquil, and the shrewd scratch out her tomb.
God, I won't let that pass.' It works, you see—
God save the King! God, somehow, free the free.

ROBIN HYDE

Sarah

The valleys, splendid as her womb,
Put forth their sons, the olive trees,
Their daughter wheat, with russet veil
Of hair resplendent to her knees.

Ever athirst, ever withheld
From the strong throes that yield up Life,
The desert shimmers in the noon,
The land named Sarah, Abram's wife;

And from her sand-dunes, tautly strung
As some great harp's unmastered chord,
Moans the harsh passion-music, wrung
In drops of blood, to please the Lord.

Where won by moisture other earth
Knits under grass to kindly clod,
My every sand-grain separate shines,
A burning-glass to draw down God,

That I may feel His lean flames run
Beneath my breasts, between my flanks,
And all the dark disturbed in me
Find voice at last, and shout Him thanks.

But great as cloud and kind as vale
Hagar moves ever in my sight—
The dark, unvext and simple loam
In which men sow their race aright;

Ploughman and harvester in turn
Have shared her wealth since time began,
And from her breasts the rivers run
That comfort still the child in man.

A curse on yearling lambs, on foals
Like wind-gusts sheathed in sorrel silk,
On heady clover, perfuming
The deep old udders dropping milk.

For locked within her, Abram's dream
Unfolds its limbs, grows fierce and tall;
And of her passive flesh he makes
His heir, the individual.

Ah, let Thy livid torrents slake
The land named Sarah! . . . Let some wild
Eclipse of reason build in me
The overthrow of Hagar's child.

113

Sisters

In a dream not long sped,
I stood on the sands, in the glassy-shattering reach of the
  waves,
Quarrelling with my sister,
And caught her arm, as in their first furious childish quarrel
Cain caught at Abel's sleeve.
Then I felt how thin her wrist was—thin as a young child's
  wrist,
Hardly more than the bones of the snowy alighting birds,
Or the mast of a boy's blue boat;
So slight the garment of flesh, thin the bone beneath,
Evanescent her young mortality.
But before I could see her eyes or speak her name,
The wave broke, covering all,
Brightening, enlarging the rock-pools.

ROBIN HYDE

from The Beaches

III

An absent face, remote and sharp, as far
As fishers' boats that bob across the bay
Setting their cray-pots in the island's shadow;
Fat men are red . . . this one's a different red,
Thin-faced and fair, burnt up in scarlet sun.

Ganges and Jumna, half the parrot places
With screeching feathers, soapstone lantern faces,
Were his; but he can't talk of what he's done.
Sometimes he hits his skull against a star,
Rages, fizzles red at everyone.

Later you hear him again: 'Sorry, old girl.'
The lamp goes up, her face looks wringing wet,
The shadow stoops, to see that we're asleep.
I'd like to ask them questions then: but one
Thinks you're clean toothbrush, homework neatly done;
One dreams, says 'A penny for a curl.'
They love you, but their thoughts tide back so deep:
Both are so very certain you'll forget.

V

This is my secret, this is the chord most perfectly strung:
There lay the dunes: I cleared them in one white stride,
Feet flying, arms flying, seagull-swift, hair and heart flying,
Smiting my feet on sand, I was into the tide:
Catching, striking, and streaming the harp-chords: for I was
    young.

This in a sea-cleft bony with old spars staring out
From the rocks and the swaying livid anemones:
But the tide broke in, and with one magnificent shout
Caught me, carried me, balanced me, held by the knees:
Curled to me, high by the wrecked and foaming trees.

But the sparkling Sabine love three moments over
Ran I and laughed, from the greenbeards' following wrath:
Whirling in winds and taunted, my hollow retreating lover

Snarled at the cliffs, as his spray-drenched hands reached
   forth:
And in many a sucking cavern, the convex eyes peered
   forth.

Turned I, and shaken, a child and a woman, blindly
Shook off the weed from my breasts, and knelt upon stone:
And climbed in the yellow steeps of a hill that held me kindly,
And lay in the yellow flowers: and lay alone:
I parted the yellow flowers and lay alone.

VI

Close under here, I watched two lovers once,
Which should have been a sin, from what you say:
I'd come to look for prawns, small pale-green ghosts,
Sea-coloured bodies tickling round the pool.
But tide was out then; so I strolled away
And climbed the dunes, to lie here warm, face down,
Watching the swimmers by the jetty-posts
And wrinkling like the bright blue wrinkling bay.
It wasn't long before they came; a fool
Could see they had to kiss; but your pet dunce
Didn't quite know men count on more than that;
And so just lay, patterning the sand.
                        And they
Were pale thin people, not often clear of town;
Elastic snapped, when he jerked off her hat;
I heard her arguing, 'Dick, my frock!' But he
Thought she was bread.
I wished her legs were brown,
And mostly, then, stared at the dawdling sea,
Hoping Perry would row me some day in his boat.

Not all the time; and when they'd gone, I went
Down to the hollow place where they had been,
Trickling bed through fingers. But I never meant
To tell the rest, or you, what I had seen;
Though that night, when I came in late for tea,
I hoped you'd see the sandgrains on my coat.

ROBIN HYDE

from The Houses

III

Adolicus; that's a creeper rug, its small
Pink-and-white piecemeal flowers swarm down a fence:
So little, no scent to be by; show, pretence—
Nothing to do, but hide the rotting wall.
Three slats were broken: but the street-boys' eyes
Can't climb in here like ants and frighten us.
Stare if they like: we've the adolicus.

VI

Section and brick and grass;
The boys lingering home from school,
Tall girls, their long hair in plaits,
Their print frocks summer cool;
Gates creaking, doors pushed ajar,
Narrow blue panes of glass;
The shabby dreamers that pass,
Afar and afar
Spilling into this city, the sunset vats.

Oven, gas-light and sink,
The cracked plates getting hot,
The tired man's tedious return
To the house that honours him not.
Singsong of lessons; the girls
Spell out their tables; food
His own, and he knows it good:
But his dry cold senses yearn
For a friendly wine to drink,
For a laugh in his dwelling-place:
Weary his woman's face,
The bitter smoke whirls.

ROBIN HYDE

from The People

I

After we'd left off loving, long after that,
When you'd not see how we were sullenly young
Nor we how you were herded 'after the war';
When staring flower stuck out a china tongue,
And door was spring and slam—not any more
The wooden friend that watched us in and out,
Storing us up as light lies stored in a tree—
Still there were words and looks that struggled free.

But most, some wound stayed wide in us; you'd changed
Fearfully: why should we let this tall man in?
Tramps come like this, come sneak-bold past the kennel;
Their dusty shirts stink—loafing there in fennel

Feathered, high-arched, with half-sweet aniseed stink!
They beg, but never flinch from what you think;
Pink passion-flowers tap them, overhead:
And so you punish them with crusts of bread,
Your neat hands fold up water from the sink;
That'll teach their smirk to mock the linen sheet!
No—there's a difference: tramps are not estranged,
They never had: they don't plant cobbly feet
And their own doorways curse them, as if for sin:
But when you passed the spindling cherry-tree
Its ghostly hailstones shivered: 'Not he! Not he!'

Lamplight: Grace requires blessings on us all:
You didn't move or speak, but I could see
In your face (and vanished before the cat could blink,)
Black riverbeds; a strange new waterfall.

II

How she grew old happened in fine-darned places,
Cracked pictures, seen too close; you'd barely know . . .
She was a red-haired woman, two little lines
Sharp cut between her brows: her eyes looked tired
As long as I remember, and her strong mouth sad.
Still she held firmly: when we went for walks
It was I who flagged: You'd never guess what frocks
She made us, while the clean thread broke and broke,
And I stood pricking at red sateen, or spoke
Roughly: that dance, the only one we had,
I remember Judy's frock of petals, wired
Bright blue, with silver wrappings round the stalks.
Sometimes I loved her: but I liked the smooth faces
Like the other mothers had, and told her so.

She laughed: she was never frightened: she took knocks
Square on the mouth, and wouldn't hit you back:
I never saw my mother dressed in black
But grief came . . . and she never let it go.

IV

But letting go . . . hands, eyes, teeth, body, all ways
A woman has of feeling proudly made . . .
Might still have left a dipping road; blue haze
(Kingfisher, sometimes), quilting soft afternoon;
But there were we, sprawled out: she was afraid,
Seeing us spring like mushrooms, big so soon;
Toadstools, perhaps she thought; her linen praise
God knows she earned; but hid it in her press,
Fearing to soil it with some bitterness
Against these young, who roared by different ways,
Drank new wine, breathed a different-seeming air;
Once she had liked her hands, but now no more
Her pride kept up its make in waist or hair:
Honour meant most. She listened by the door
For who'd betray it; but too spent to care.

ROBIN HYDE

Journey from New Zealand

Now as I go between sands red and yellow as poppies,
Or across a desert many-breasted like Kali,
Shifting, changing, with navels and sockets of wet deep blue,
I shall see always these things, patient yet obdurate,
And my heart be broken for them, as together we wait the
    rainfall.

120

Earth, earth, and the purple thither-dusty grasses,
I shall dream thee fat rains, waiting alone by the desert
Whose white and bitter body makes mock of rain.
Sheep bought for Russia, thick-sided breeding rams
With the grey grass of the steppes tangled between your
   teeth,
Do you lift up your heads, short and bellicose, black-nosed,
With the round horns curled hard as a boxer's fist?
Do you lift up your heads, snuffing their north-watered
   wind
That drank ice each winter, and seek, however dimly,
The scent of another spring than the Muscovy spring?
(Down in Mackenzie Country
They burn off tussock each year, with the writhing flares
Tied to their galloping horses' tails.)
You cannot remember the snow-fence, black birch rotting in
   slabs,
Or your weak protesting cries
As Old Donald, the shepherd, snuggled you into his plaid,
And blinking stiff lashes free, thanked his stiff God
For a new lamb, delivered alive in snowtime.
The bark and frisking of collies is gone from you,
Lost honey, dissolved in the vague old murmuring hives of
   your brain,
Yet, as you lift your heads snuffing, (the train growls by,)
I have a hope you will find their grass acrid, will give
Some maimed defiance out of the weight of your loins.
I too am sold into strangeness,
I too will look out of windows, thinking 'How fair!' or
   'Strange . . .'
(Is ringo their word for an apple?)
But in my heart will only dissolve, re-form,
The circling shapes of familiar things.

That place trodden hard,
With the white cocks pecking in the sun,
Their combs like dusty blood,
Under the pines, and the serious pungent macrocarpa,
Don't we all know it?

Those dropped shafts of a gig
Leathered over from rain; (it is seldom used now,
Seldom the jolting and laughing into market,
One boot high on the high old iron step,
And jogging in front the mare, the solemn dappled buttocks,
Black tail lifted for clean manure,
Grizzled lashes winking over her eyes,
Part of a world still—cars or no cars):
Ah, I shall speak it between the scorching beats of the train.
(Change for Berlin midnight!)

Watching the kea, red outlaw, circle a plain
Scarred with river-beds, where gorse-gold metal
Flares up at the copper metal of underwings;
I climbed a snow-peak once; who would believe
How the ribbed gold grass bowed frozen into the snow?
How a fall sprang out and down, singing,
The mountain's woman,
And the dreadful singing of winds blew forth at dark?
Down upon Diamond Lake, the trout plopped home
Spreading such lonely circles;
The dying boy mined scheelite,
And the old man polished his well-loved worthless greenstone.

They say the great bird still stalks at Manapouri;
No one has tramped those Sounds.
They speak of great men with red beards;
(Quickly; this gulping train must start at midnight).

Your crude country, hard as unbroken shell . . .
She was hard to love, and took strength, like a virgin.
Sometimes, in money or dust, the little farms ebbed away,
Dripping between disconsolate fingers like blood
Of that harsh girl, who would never love you.
But in the cities (old days!)
We could live better, warm and safe as the sparrows,
Twittering through the evenings like young sparrows.
Ours was a city, like any city,
But with more, perhaps, of sea and cloud, not long loved.

November tar, ripening, blackened our sandals.
Our city had doorways, too many shut.
Morning and evening, facing the rampant crimson brutes of
    the light,
Nobody had the beautiful strength to decree:
'Leave your doors open morning and evening—
Leave your gates wide to the stranger.'
So ours was a city, like any city, but fair.
At seven (still light), the children snuggled down
Like rabbits. The rest sat on in the lamplight,
Sat still or spoke words by their failures.

There is nothing else to tell, but the catkin grass
Strung on pale wires, close to the sea.
Our great rocks fluked like whales,
We loved the dead coal-hulks, did not despise them.
Money was nothing, balloons were much.
The grey mists quiet-breasted as doves.

I knew a green place where the light looked more like trees,
Trees more like diffused and stilly light.

123

(Green, green be upon your eyes; red in my heart,
The world's troubled colour; for I must awaken.)
Once in the rose parterres, my mother stood still and said:
'Man, woman and child; man, woman and child.'
She was born with a restive heart, but grew old.

Ah, too many sparrows twittering in the dawn . . .
The deep, blue and unborn colour.
The dawn should be men's, not your little voices.
It was always too soon to awake, I remember now,
But the world, this and that world,
And the Templar stars in their order said: 'Rise and go.'

ROBIN HYDE

Ku Li

Two words from China: 'Ku li'—bitter strength.
'This coolies' war!' tinkle the sweet-belled idle.
His face and Hundred Names sweep on below,
Child-like, he plays at horse without the bridle:
And carts a world along, and carts a war,
Tugging perhaps to mountain heights at length:
The new vernacular chronicles exhort him,
And waste their breath.
His grinning face can't know
Half the fixed meanings of the flags he saw:
He had a happy childhood: then time caught him,
Broadened his shoulders, but forbore his head.

124

Eight years his life between the shafts: eight hours
(With luck), between Changsha and Hsuchowfu,
Picks swinging like pendulums in a noon of flowers:
Shining their freedom, bombers spot his blue,
But cease to count. Too poor for marriage-bed
He looks for dreaming in the big dim shed,
Rolled in the quilt where other warmth has dossed:

Turns to Yunnan, hacks the next strategy through,
Cheerful; and often killed; and always bossed.
And not on Tiger Head or Purple Mountain
His grave-mound rises: worlds live on, to slake
Their ashy gullets at his bitter fountain
Of blood and vigour. Enemy armies break
Somehow on this, as somehow cracks the stone
Under his pick: but now he rots alone
(Not claiming to have died for something's sake,)
Only the earth makes ready for his bone,
The green rice sees him with unflattering eyes:
Too cheap a partisan for man to prize,
Men seldom know him for their broadest river,
And burnt in the immortal tiles forever.

DOUGLAS STEWART

Mending the Bridge

Burnished with copper light, burnished,
The men are brutal: their bodies jut out square,
Massive as rock in the lanterns' stormy glare
Against the devastation of the dark.

Now passionate, as if to gouge the stark
Quarry of baleful light still deeper there,
With slow gigantic chopping rhythm they hack
Beat back and crumple up and spurn the black
Live night, the marsh-black sludgy air.

And clamour the colour of copper light
Swings from their hammering and speeds and breaks
Darkness to clots and spattering light, and flakes
Oily, like dazzling snow and storms of oil.
The night, that never sleeps, quickens. The soil
The stones and the grass are alive. The thrush awakes,
Huddles and finds the leaves gone hard and cool.
The cows in the fields are awake, restless; the bull
Restless. The dogs. A young horse snorts and shakes.

Beneath the square of glaring light
The river still is muttering of flood,
The dark day when thick with ugly mud,
Swirling with logs and swollen beasts (and some
Still alive, drowning) it had come
Snarling, a foul beast chewing living cud,
And grappled with the bridge and tried to rend it,
So now these stronger brutes must sweat to mend it,
Labouring in light like orange blood.

Men labour in the city so,
With naked fore-arms singed with copper light,
And strangeness on them as with stone they fight,
Each meet for fear, and even the curt drill
Mysterious as trees and a dark hill.
But these are stronger, these oppose their might
To storm and flood and all the land's black power.
Burnished with sweat and lanterns now they tower
Monstrous against the marshes of the night.

DOUGLAS STEWART

Green Lions

The bay is gouged by the wind.
In the jagged hollows green lions crouch,
And stretch,
And slouch,
And sudden with spurting manes and a glitter of haunches
Charge at the shore
And rend the sand and roar.

And inland, in offices and banks
Though trams clang down and heavy stone resists
The mutter of distant carnage still persists,
And men denied the jungle of young years

Grow taut, and clench their fists.

DENIS GLOVER

Home Thoughts

In Windsor Castle lives the king.
No doubt it is a pleasant thing
To sing of Windsor and the king,
But if I sing of anything
I much prefer to sing of where
The tram-cars clang across the square,
Or where above the little bay
John Robert Godley passed his day,
Or where the brooding hills reveal
The sunset as a living weal.

I think, too, of the bridle-track
Where first they saw the plains curve back
To Alps, of how that little band
Of pilgrims viewed their Promised Land.

For I am glad when new lands yield
Their stubborn crust to living field,
And when the road goes scarring back
Through silence to a mountain shack
Where blankets, candles, frying-pan
Bespeak the only needs of man.

I do not dream of Sussex downs
Or quaint old England's quaint old towns:
I think of what will yet be seen
In Johnsonville and Geraldine.

DENIS GLOVER

The Magpies

When Tom and Elizabeth took the farm
The bracken made their bed,
And *Quardle oodle ardle wardle doodle*
The magpies said.

Tom's hand was strong to the plough
Elizabeth's lips were red,
And *Quardle oodle ardle wardle doodle*
The magpies said.

Year in year out they worked
While the pines grew overhead,
And *Quardle oodle ardle wardle doodle*
The magpies said.

Elizabeth is dead now (it's years ago);
Old Tom went light in the head;
And *Quardle oodle ardle wardle doodle*
The magpies said.

The farm's still there. Mortgage corporations
Couldn't give it away.
And *Quardle oodle ardle wardle doodle*
The magpies say.

DENIS GLOVER

Arrowtown

Gold in the hills, gold in the rocks,
Gold in the river gravel,
Gold as yellow as Chinamen
In the bottom of the shovel.

Gold built the bank its sham façade;
Behind that studded door
Gold dribbled over the counter
Into the cracks of the floor.

Gold pollinated the whole town;
But the golden bees are gone—
Now round a country butcher's shop
The sullen blowflies drone,

Now paved with common clay
Are the roads of Arrowtown;
And the silt of the river is grey
In the golden sun.

Threnody

In Plimmerton, in Plimmerton,
The little penguins play,
And one dead albatross was found
At Karehana Bay.

In Plimmerton, in Plimmerton,
The seabirds haunt the cave,
And often in the summertime
The penguins ride the wave.

In Plimmerton, in Plimmerton,
The penguins live, they say,
But one dead albatross they found
At Karehana Bay.

DENIS GLOVER

Waitaki Dam

Making mountain war, here river wandered
With no easy gait or broad assurance.
Tunnelling the high hill's heart, scouring at clay,
Torn waters snouted earth, roared in ravine,
Swung potently against the fathomed bluff.

Stronger than this, eyes' focussed wedge
Laid bare the river's bed, measured the mountain,
Mortared the shattered rock, and built the dam.

Moon now hangs white over the altered scene
Where stars reflect themselves and nightbound bird
Dips as the wavelets lap low island mounds.
The traveller's heart lifts at enchanted change.

Making new contours, drowning tree and crop.
Filling the empty air between the hills
With quiet inundation, lies the lake.
The peace of water settles over the hills.

Slow water sails towards a blinding brink,
One moment at the brink timeless it hangs,
Creams over the lip, carpets the smooth slope,
Joyously leaps, and—shattered, troubled air
Trembling with music where the blown spray hangs—
Thunders to freedom in the pool below.

On broken earth nearby small houses perch,
And nursling trees and small transplanted flowers
Precariously root in trampled clay.
Heat holds the township, or the winter frost.
But always water rushes to the brink,
The harnessed races give their singing power
And after long internment in the hills
The river smoothly slides away to sea.

DENIS GLOVER

Dunedin Revisited

A mountain like a beast
Is crouched in the north
(Where there is only trouble
And the political bubble.)

To the south
Lies a great river's mouth.

Under Flagstaff's boulders
Beds the town; and the houses
Complacent over one another's shoulders
Look on a harbour pleasant as a pond
—With gate-crashing rollers just beyond
Where remotely the sugared island still
Winters in the Pacific's hug and maul.

Over the harbour waters
A slow-gonged clock
Floats the hours and the quarters.

From the quarry, all day without shock
Comes the hill-deadened, water-damped
Sound of explosions; and haunting
The frost-quiet of midnight
The redundant the echoing
Bull-breath of shunting.

More eloquent than speech
In probing the dreamlike past
And answering the reproach
By time's soft-fingered shadow cast,
The spires fly heavenward.

A long sunset spills
On those returning,
And the manuka hills
Know the slow smoke of burning.

132

DENIS GLOVER

Drift

Drift drift upon the beach
Dead Man's Bay and Dead Man's Reach
Driftwood dunks and driftwood rides
Inert upon the endless tides
Debris down the river drifting
Debris of the ocean's sifting
Sullen log the sodden boot
Tangled in the mangrove root
Upturned boat and empty tin
Drifting out and drifting in
One storm took them one storm more
May drive them to the indifferent shore
Castaways of wind and weather
Drifting aimlessly together.

DENIS GLOVER

For a Child

Cave Rock is made of toffee
And the sea of lemonade
And the little waitress wavelets
Are always on parade
    When the cars roll down to Sumner
    On a Sunday.

The ice-cream mountain on the blue
Is free for anyone,
And Scarborough Head looms solid
As a tearoom tuppenny bun
        When mum and dad look glum or glad
        At Sumner on a Sunday.

And wistfully the children sit
While Army trombones teach
That only Christ, not Cortes,
Can land upon the beach
        At Sumner when the seas roll in,
        At Sumner on a Sunday.

DENIS GLOVER

To a Woman

Though the world is torn with care
I am here, and you are here.

We are two, but we are one
When the world leaves us alone;

Nowhere is there less distress
Than in the frolic of your dress;

But nowhere on a pillow is
More than a destroying bliss

And nowhere is there more despair
Than in the tangle of your hair.

134

DENIS GLOVER

Security

In these far cleaner days no armies clash:
Here's the quick spurt of fire, the sudden crash.

Upon the buildings' battlements the flags
Of all the nations warn off all the birds.
No thoughts are wasted by the lookouts waiting
For the pulsing far-off drone or the bomb-baiting.

Our tanks (alas too few) rumble the city street
And troops clump off to where machine-guns meet.
Someone has blundered: transport being short
The laden infantry perforce must walk.

Loudspeakers hourly give the news its news,
Exhorting calm and patience to the patient queues.

The calm and patient guns, daylight and dark,
While waiting gunners yawn, sleep in the park—
The radar dawn will warn of the approach
When egg-like buildings burn and pavements poach.

Again the loudspeaker, speaking through woollen socks,
Exhorts for God, for freedom, and the ballot box.

Off Banks Peninsula

Clear and sweet in the crystal weather
The sail and the shroud
Are walking and talking together.

Wind tumbles from the sail, the blocks
Clattering, and the hull dies.

To drift at the cliff's foot
Is to feel the south. The swell
Heaves wide and free like a mature woman,
And the rocks,
Bannered with weed among the gulph
And tumour of the tide
Accept with patience each long kiss.

The far brown hills swelling triumphant
From the plain of blue to the blue sky
Bosom the easy cloud,
Serene and self-possessed rising
Amid illimitable seas endlessly sad.

Wind whispers in: and the yacht again
Asserts direction on the trackless tide.

DENIS GLOVER

In the Township

Said Lizzie the big blonde barmaid, 'There,'
She said to the man at the bar,
'There he is still—it's old
Arawata Bill off looking for gold,'

With grub in his saddlebag
And baccy in his pouch
Arawata Bill headed for the Woodhen gulch.

'He's half-crazed y'know,
Always on the go
—But the only gold he'll ever pan
Is the glitter in his eyes
If you know what I mean.'

Where is the riverflat
Where colour shows in the shovel
And nuggets as big as berries are found
Burgeoning in the gravel?

'—Comes in with an ounce or two
Sometimes, and goes on the spree,
But there's no talking to the man
He's that far away,

Except with one or two in,
When he'll sing and he'll holler
As good as the best,
Dancing to the victrola.'

Now I've never tried
From the head of the Arawata
To the divide and down
To the Dart on the other side.

'Next day he'd go, whether it
Rained or froze.
You'd almost believe
There was something in those
God-forsaken hills he couldn't leave.

Yes, he's a queer one
And not what you might call
Sociable-like—and truth to tell
I expect there's a woman behind it all.'

Arawata Bill led his horse up the slow hill
And his shovel was lashed to his pack.

DENIS GLOVER

Songs

I

These songs will not stand—
The wind and the sand will smother.

Not I but another
Will make songs worth the bother:

The rimu or kauri he,
I'm but the cabbage tree,

Sings Harry to an old guitar.

138

If everywhere in the street
Is the indifferent, the accustomed eye
Nothing can elate,
It's nothing to do with me,
   Sings Harry in the wind-break.

To the north are islands like stars
In the blue water
And south, in that crystal air,
The ice-floes grind and mutter,
   Sings Harry in the wind-break.

At one flank old Tasman, the boar,
Slashes and tears,
And the other Pacific's sheer
Mountainous anger devours,
   Sings Harry in the wind-break.

From the cliff-top a boy
Felt that great motion,
And pupil to the horizon's eye
Grew wide with vision,
   Sings Harry in the wind-break.

But grew to own fences barbed
Like the words of a quarrel;
And the sea never disturbed
Him fat as a barrel,
   Sings Harry in the wind-break.

Who once would gather all Pacific
In a net wide as his heart
Soon is content to watch the traffic
Or lake waves breaking short,
   Sings Harry in the wind-break.

I Remember

I remember paddocks opening green
On mountains tussock-brown,
And the rim of fire on the hills,
And the river running down;

And the smoke of the burning scrub,
And my two uncles tall,
And the smell of earth new-ploughed,
And the antlers in the hall,
                              Sings Harry.

Then Uncle Jim was off to the wars
With a carbine at his saddle
And was killed in the Transvaal
—I forget in just what battle.

And Uncle Simon left the farm
After some wild quarrel,
Rolled his blanket and rode off
Whistling on his sorrel.

My father held to the land
Running good cattle there,
And I grew up like a shaggy steer
And as swift as a hare
While the river ran down.

But that was long ago
When the hawk hovered over the hill
And the deer lifted their heads
And a boy lay still
By the river running down.
                              Sings Harry.

DENIS GLOVER

Once the Days

Once the days were clear
Like mountains in water,
The mountains were always there
And the mountain water;

And I was a fool leaving
Good land to moulder,
Leaving the fences sagging
And the old man older
To follow my wild thoughts
Away over the hill,
Where there is only the world
And the world's ill,
                              sings Harry.

DENIS GLOVER

Lake, Mountain, Tree

Water brimmed against the shore
Oozing among the reeds,
And looking into the lake I saw
Myself and mountains and weeds.

From the crystal uttermost ridge
Dwarfed was the river's course;
Cloud-shouting, to the world's edge
I rode a whole island for my horse.

Forlorn at the last tree,
Grey shingle bruised our bones;
But there holding tenaciously
Were roots among stones.

Knowing less now, and alone,
These things make for me
A gauge to measure the unknown
—Lake, mountain, tree,

sings Harry.

DENIS GLOVER

The Casual Man

Come, mint me up the golden gorse,
Mine me the yellow clay
—There's no money in my purse
For a rainy day,

sings Harry.

My father left me his old coat,
Nothing more than that;
And will my head take hurt
In an old hat?
                    sings Harry.

They all concern themselves too much
With what a clock shows.
But does the casual man care
How the world goes?
                    sings Harry.

A little here, a little there—
Why should a man worry?
Let the world hurry by,
I'll not hurry,
                    sings Harry.

DENIS GLOVER

Thistledown

Once I followed horses
And once I followed whores,
And marched once with a banner
For some great cause,
                    sings Harry.
But that was thistledown planted on the wind.

And once I met a woman
All in her heart's spring,
But I was a headstrong fool
Heedless of everything,
                    sings Harry.
—I was thistledown planted on the wind.

143

Mustering is the life:
Freed of fears and hopes
I watch the sheep like a pestilence
Pouring over the slopes,
                    sings Harry.

And the past is thistledown planted on the wind.

Dream and doubt and the deed
Dissolve like a cloud
On the hills of time.
Be a man never so proud,
                    sings Harry,

He is only thistledown planted on the wind.

DENIS GLOVER

Themes

What shall we sing? sings Harry.

Sing truthful men? Where shall we find
The man who cares to speak his mind:
Truth's out of uniform, sings Harry,
That's her offence
Where lunacy parades as commonsense.

Of lovers then? A sorry myth
To tickle tradesmen's palates with.
Production falls, wise men can prove,
When factory girls dream dreams of love.

144

Sing of our leaders? Like a pall
Proficiency descends on all
Pontific nobodies who make
Some high pronouncement every week.

Of poets then? How rarely they
Are more than summer shadow-play.
Like canvassers from door to door
The poets go, and gain no ear.

Sing of the fighters? Brave-of-Heart
Soon learns to play the coward's part,
And calls it, breaking solemn pacts,
Fair Compromise or Facing Facts.

Where all around us ancient ills
Devour like blackberry the hills
On every product of the time
Let fall a poisoned rain of rhyme,
                              sings Harry;
But praise St Francis feeding crumbs
Into the empty mouths of guns.

What shall we sing? sings Harry.

Sing all things sweet or harsh upon
These islands in the Pacific sun,
The mountains whitened endlessly
And the white horses of the winter sea,
                              sings Harry.

145

ALLEN CURNOW

'The Water is Burred with Rain'

(*from* Not in Narrow Seas)

The water is burred with rain.
Men scrape rough iron, squatting
On the slung plank, setting
Knee and toe to the ship's flank.

(There are five wharves.
Today the port is quite full.
They will load mutton and wool
As soon as the rain stops.

The Minister believes
The price is sufficient to cover
Necessaries, and something over
For a radio, perhaps a car.)

Rust and dust and the keen
Wind slapping the ankle:
Flutters the flaked waste of oceans
Cold hands carve and sprinkle
To blue-lipped silt below.

ALLEN CURNOW

'The Bishop Boundary-rides his Diocese'
(*from* Not in Narrow Seas)

The bishop boundary-rides his diocese
Carrying the sacraments at saddle-bow;
The church equestrian christens peak and river
Where land is cheap and the reapers are few.

Years after where his lordship braved the ford
Less hardy saints cross bridges in a gig:
Good rents assure their stipends, not even
Judas so providently kept the bag.

A faith worthy of empire; ere the four
Earliest migrant vessels put to sea
The wise company granted God permission
To work His passage to the colony.

Guaranteed seed in a prepared soil—
What land would not give the approved return?
Here's no renewal of the world's youth,
But age-soured infancy, a darkened dawn.

Stratagem

Fear made the superior sea
The colour of his new car;
From a window in the hillside
He saw the sky bare
All but the handhold of a cloud
On a derelict gate. Ashamed,
He knew the weedy fog showed
His mother's hair uncombed;
And all for that the snaking road
In low gear climbed.
Before night he punished them,
The bright scenes hostile,
By a boy and girl in the young broom.
He told that story well.

ALLEN CURNOW

Time

I am the nor'west air nosing among the pines
I am the water-race and the rust on railway lines
I am the mileage recorded on the yellow signs.

I am dust, I am distance, I am lupins along the beach
I am the sums the sole-charge teachers teach
I am cows called to milking and the magpie's screech.

I am nine o'clock in the morning when the office is clean
I am the slap of the belting and the smell of the machine
I am the place in the park where the lovers were seen.

I am recurrent music the children hear
I am level noises in the remembering ear
I am the sawmill and the passionate second gear.

I, Time, am all these yet these exist
Among my mountainous fabrics like a mist,
So do they the measurable world resist.

I, Time, call down, condense, confer
On the willing memory the shapes these were:
I, more than your conscious carrier,

Am island, am sea, am father, farm, and friend;
Though I am here all things my coming attend;
I am, you have heard it, the Beginning and the End.

ALLEN CURNOW

Wild Iron

Sea go dark, go dark with wind
Feet go heavy, go heavy with sand,
Thoughts go wild, go wild with the sound
Of iron on the old shed clanging,
Iron on his gallows hanging, banging.
Go dark, go heavy, go wild, go round,
  Dark with the wind
  Heavy with the sand,
Wild with the iron that tugs at the nail
And the foundering shriek of the gale.

149

ALLEN CURNOW

The Unhistoric Story

Whaling for continents suspected deep in the south
The Dutchmen envied the unknown, drew bold
Images of marketplace, populous rivermouth,
The Land of Beach ignorant of the value of gold.
    Morning in Murderers' Bay,
    Blood drifted away.
    It was something different, something
    Nobody counted on.

Spider, clever and fragile, Cook showed how
To spring a trap for islands, turning from planets
His measuring mission, showed what the musket could do,
Made his Christmas goose of the wild gannets;
    Still as the collier steered
    No continent appeared;
    It was something different, something
    Nobody counted on.

The roving tentacles rested, touched, clutched
Substantial earth, that is, accustomed haven
For the hungry whaler. Some inland, some hutched
Rudely in bays, the shaggy foreshore shaven,
    Lusted, preached as they knew,
    But as the children grew
    It was something different, something
    Nobody counted on.

Green slashed with flags, pipeclay and boots in the bush,
Christ in canoes and the musketed Maori boast;
All a rubble-rattle at Time's glacial push:
Vogel and Seddon howling empire from an empty coast
    A vast ocean laughter
    Echoed unheard, and after
    All it was different, something
    Nobody counted on.

The pilgrim dream pricked by a cold dawn died
Among the chemical farmers, the fresh towns; among
Miners, not husbandmen, who piercing the side
Let the land's life, found like all who had so long
    Bloodily or tenderly striven
    To rearrange the given,
    It was something different, something
    Nobody counted on.

After all re-ordering of old elements
Time trips up all but the humblest of heart
Stumbling after the fire, not in the smoke of events;
For many are called, but many are left at the start,
    And whatever islands may be
    Under or over the sea,
    It is something different, something
    Nobody counted on.

ALLEN CURNOW

Crash at Leithfield

O ruinous morning, unjustifiable
Even in the facile logic of defence;
Death neither splendid nor ignoble,
Rashness at best, at worst incompetence.

Low he flew, inexpert nerve straining,
Lens-curved Pegasus Bay—more Icarus he
Raw to wings made trial of his training
Thirty miles on the white seam of land and sea.

Leithfield and lupins, lower, till the roar
Lay flat as a tractor on the brackish land,
Stiffly gasping at each gust of the nor'
Wester. Imminence of engine's sound

Started eyes darting up in township and farm;
Suddenly machine turned man between earth and sun,
Struggling in sucking airs. Could ignorant alarm
Read in his wingtips what was urgent to be done?

Lower, like bird in wave-trough, gustily rearing
Inland, wing flashed sunnily; steep and slow
O his wild banking had the farm women fearing
What faith in their darling's daring might undergo.

Did he know before they knew the instant had passed
When a touch might start the capable smooth climb?
Did he know which deafening second was the last?
Was there pause in purpose, then the downthrust of Time?

Steadily, gaily tilted to the sun, droning
Still under power, engine and gale together,
To naively cruel earth too swift declining,
To the haystack's and the gum-tree's windy weather;

And the crash, how queerly gentle, how cool the cloud
Black-billowing like loam, and silent—
Ah, silence queerer than all—how small, not loud
When this was, we thought, to have been so violent.

And they were still sitting in the aeroplane
Said the baker's driver who sped to be in at the kill,
While it was burning; he said again and again
Both of them were sitting, they are sitting there still.

Some took home bits of scorched fabric and some
Said they thought he was trying to land, and all that day
We watched or heard aircraft after aircraft come
Like foul birds over the dead, and none to drive them away.

ALLEN CURNOW

House and Land

Wasn't this the site, asked the historian,
Of the original homestead?
Couldn't tell you, said the cowman;
I just live here, he said,
Working for old Miss Wilson,
Since the old man's been dead.

Moping under the bluegums
The dog trailed his chain
From the privy as far as the fowlhouse
And back to the privy again,
Feeling the stagnant afternoon
Quicken with the smell of rain.

There sat old Miss Wilson,
With her pictures on the wall,
The baronet uncle, mother's side,
And one she called The Hall;
Taking tea from a silver pot
For fear the house might fall.

She's all of eighty said the cowman
Down at the milking-shed.
I'm leaving here next winter,
Too bloody quiet he said.

The spirit of exile, wrote the historian,
Is strong in the people still.

He reminds me rather, said Miss Wilson,
Of Harriet's youngest, Will.

The cowman, home from the shed, went drinking
With the rabbiter home from the hill.

The sensitive nor'west afternoon
Collapsed, and the rain came;
The dog crept into his barrel,
Looking lost and lame.
But you can't attribute to either
Awareness of what great gloom
Stands in a land of settlers
With never a soul at home.

ALLEN CURNOW

Country School
North Canterbury

You know the school; you call it old—
Scrub-worn floors and paint all peeled
On barge-board, weatherboard, and gibbet belfry.

Pinus betrays, with rank tufts topping
The roof-ridge, scattering bravely
Nor'west gale as a reef its waves
While little girls squeal at skipping
And magpies hoot from the eaves:

For scantling Pinus stands mature
In less than the life of a man;
The rusty saplings, the school, and you
Together your lives began.

O sweet antiquity! Look, the stone
That skinned your knees. How small
Are the terrible doors; how sad the dunny
And the things you drew on the wall.

ALLEN CURNOW

Magellan

Horizon's hatred smites Magellan,
Parched in Pacific, scurvy-swollen;

Men and ships all the mild weather
Share one rhythm and rot together,

In festering flesh, in softening wood,
Brine is sap and brine is blood;

Vain the Virgin on clotted tongue;
The dead dive where the dead belong

Whose mutinous limbs dissolving down
Lighten the keels of Christian Spain:

Pluck wave at plank, blaze sun in sky,
Magellan shall have land with joy,

Shall forge for fetter on the seas
Tally of his tormented days.

ALLEN CURNOW

Landfall in Unknown Seas

*The 300th Anniversary of the Discovery of New Zealand
by Abel Tasman, 13 December 1642*

I

Simply by sailing in a new direction
You could enlarge the world.

                You picked your captain,
Keen on discoveries, tough enough to make them,
Whatever vessels could be spared from other
More urgent service for a year's adventure;
Took stock of the more probable conjectures
About the Unknown to be traversed, all
Guesses at golden coasts and tales of monsters
To be digested into plain instructions
For likely and unlikely situations.

156

All this resolved and done, you launched the whole
On a fine morning, the best time of year,
Skies widening and the oceanic furies
Subdued by summer illumination; time
To go and to be gazed at going
On a fine morning, in the Name of God
Into the nameless waters of the world.

O you had estimated all the chances
Of business in those waters, the world's waters
Yet unexploited.
                    But more than the sea-empire's
Cannon, the dogs of bronze and iron barking
From Timor to the Straits, backed up the challenge.
Between you and the South an older enmity
Lodged in the searching mind, that would not tolerate
So huge a hegemony of ignorance.
There, where your Indies had already sprinkled
Their tribes like ocean rains, you aimed your voyage;
Like them invoked your God, gave seas to history
And islands to new hazardous tomorrows.

II

Suddenly exhilaration
Went off like a gun, the whole
Horizon, the long chase done,
Hove to. There was the seascape
Crammed with coast, surprising
As new lands will, the sailor
Moving on the face of the waters,
Watching the earth take shape
Round the unearthly summits, brighter
Than its emerging colour.

157

Yet this, no far fool's errand,
Was less than the heart desired,
In its old Indian dream
The glittering gulfs ascending
Past palaces and mountains
Making one architecture.
Here the uplifted structure,
Peak and pillar of cloud—
O splendour of desolation—reared
Tall from the pit of the swell,
With a shadow, a finger of wind, forbade
Hopes of a lucky landing.

Always to islanders danger
Is what comes over the sea;
Over the yellow sands and the clear
Shallows, the dull filament
Flickers, the blood of strangers:
Death discovered the Sailor
O in a flash, in a flat calm
A clash of boats in the bay
And the day marred with murder.
The dead required no further
Warning to keep their distance;
The rest, noting the failure,
Pushed on with a reconnaissance
To the north; and sailed away.

III

Well, home is the Sailor, and that is a chapter
In a schoolbook, a relevant yesterday
We thought we knew all about, being much apter
    To profit, sure of our ground,
No murderers mooring in our Golden Bay.

But now there are no more islands to be found
And the eye scans risky horizons of its own
In unsettled weather, and murmurs of the drowned
     Haunt their familiar beaches—
Who navigates us towards what unknown

But not improbable provinces? Who reaches
A future down for us from the high shelf
Of spiritual daring? Not those speeches
     Pinning on the Past like a decoration
For merit that congratulates itself,

O not the self-important celebration
Or most painstaking history, can release
The current of a discoverer's elation
     And silence the voices saying,
'Here is the world's end where wonders cease.'

Only by a more faithful memory, laying
On him the half-light of a diffident glory,
The Sailor lives, and stands beside us, paying
     Out into our time's wave
The stain of blood that writes an island story.

ALLEN CURNOW

Attitudes for a New Zealand Poet: III
(*The skeleton of the Great Moa in the Canterbury Museum,
Christchurch*)

The skeleton of the moa on iron crutches
Figures in no waste land; a private swamp
Was where this tree grew feathers once, that hatches
Its broods of dust, and guards them from the damp.

Interesting failure to adapt on islands,
Taller but not more fallen than I, who come
Bone to his bone, peculiarly New Zealand's.
The eyes of children flicker round this tomb

Under the skylights, wonder at the huge egg
Found in a thousand pieces, pieced together
But with less patience than the bones that dug
In time deep shelter against ocean weather.

Not I, some child, born in a marvellous year,
Will learn the trick of standing upright here.

ALLEN CURNOW

Out of Sleep

Awake but not yet up, too early morning
Brings you like bells in matrix of mist
Noises the mind may finger, but no meaning.
Two blocks away a single car has crossed

Your intersection with the hour; each noise
A cough in the cathedral of your waking—
The cleaners have no souls, no sins—each does
Some job, Christ dying or the day breaking.

This you suppose is what goes on all day.
No-one is allowed long to stop and listen,
But takes brief turns at it: now as you lie
Dead calm, a gust in the damp cedar hissing

Will have the mist right off in half a minute.
You will not grasp the meaning, you will be in it.

ALLEN CURNOW

At Dead Low Water
Governor's Bay, December 1944

I

At dead low water, smell of harbour bottom,
Sump of opulent tides; in foul chinks twirl
Weed and whorl of silt recoiling, clouding
The wan harbour sighing on all its beaches.

The boat was not deliberately abandoned
But tied here and forgotten, left afloat
Freakishly, bobbing where the summers foundered,
Jarring each wave the jetty's tettered limbs;

Worm carves wave polishes original shapes,
Bolt and knot give way, gaps in the decking
Turn up again, driftwood on other sands.
All drifts, till fire or burial.

Life, trapped, remembers in the rancid shallows
What crept before the enormous strides of love
When the Word alone was, and the waters:
Goes back to the beginning, the whole terror

Of time and patience. Keel and bolt are frilled
With the shrimp's forest, all green-bearded timbers.
Salt rocky chink, nude silted cleft give off
Birth smell, death smell. Mute ages tread the womb.

Nervous quiet not calm possesses
Sea water here, the wave turns wary
Finding itself so far inland.

The father with the child came down
First thing one morning, before any
Dreamt of visiting the beach; it was

Daylight but grey, midsummer; they
Crossed high-water mark, dry-shod,
Derelict shells, weed crisped or rotting,

Down to the spongy rim, slowly
Without fear, stepping hand in hand
Within an inch of the harmless sea

Pure, unfractured, many miles,
Still steel water sheathed between
Once violent hills, volcanic shapes.

O memory, child, what entered at the
Eye, ecstasy, air or water?
What at the mouth? But carefully

Morning by morning incorruption
Puts on corruption; nervously
Wave creeps in and lingers over

Tideswept heaps where the fly breeds:
Memory flows where all is tainted,
Death with life and life with death.

Twenty years. A child returned
Discerns in quicksand his own footprint
Brimming and fading, vanishing.

III

Failed at the one flood, we do not count
On miracles again, and you may say
We die from now: while each amazed migrant
Waves back, and cannot tear his eyes away

From his own image, the weeping threatening
Accusing thing, and knows death does not rid
Him even of the deformed sunk sifted thing,
Memory's residue; because the dead,

Father and child, still walk the water's edge:
A kindness, an inconsequent pastime, froze
In time's tormented rock, became an age
When tropics shifted, buried rivers rose,

Meaningless but for individual pain
No death, no birth relieves or lunar pulses drown.

ALLEN CURNOW

Elegy on My Father

Tremayne Curnow, of Canterbury, New Zealand, 1880–1949

Spring in his death abounds among the lily islands,
There to bathe him for the grave antipodean snows
Fall floodlong, rivermouths all in bloom, and those
Fragile church timbers quiver
By the bourne of his burial where robed he goes
No journey at all. One sheet's enough to cover
My end of the world and his, and the same silence.

While in Paddington autumn is air-borne, earth-given,
Day's nimbus nearer staring, colder smoulders;
Breath of a death not my own bewilders
Dead calm with breathless choirs
O bird-creation singing where the world moulders!
God's poor, the crutched and stunted spires
Thumb heavenward humorously under the unriven

Marble November has nailed across their sky:
Up there, dank ceiling is the dazzling floor
All souls inhabit, the lilied seas, no shore
My tear-smudged map mislimned.
When did a wind of the extreme South before
Mix autumn, spring, and death? False maps are dimmed,
Lovingly they mock each other, image and eye.

The ends of the earth are folded into his grave
In sound of the Pacific and the hills he travelled singing;
For he ferried like a feather the crushing dream, bringing
The Word, the Wine, the Bread.
Some bell down the obliterating gale was ringing
To the desert the visiting glory; dust he trod
Gathered its grains for a miracle, and the nave

He knelt in put off its poor planks, loomed loftier,
Lonelier than Losinga's that spells in stone
The Undivided Name. O quickening bone
Of the masspriest, under grass
Green in my absent Spring, sweet relic atone
To our Lord's earth for the pride of all our voyages,
That the salt winds which scattered us blow softer.

CHARLES BRASCH

Crossing the Straits

You that nightly cross the straits,
For whom a darkened island waits
To start with daybreak up from sea
Actual, proven; whom the wet quay
And shunned grey streets conduct to some
Transforming oracular rite; and whom
The city at last silences
And drowns, unwilling to set eyes
Upon its victims, after breaking
Every promise spoken, or speaking
In false smiling;—you that crossed,
Burning, in the silent post-
haste ferry: what great promise hung
Above the dark island, what tongue
Uttered out of night what word,
To draw like a migrating bird
You fearless over?
                 For no light
Can pup those promises of night,
Substance, and creature; no, nor give
Yesterday's wantless world alive
Again, nor pass across the straits
You, whom no darkened island waits.

CHARLES BRASCH

A View of Rangitoto

Harshness of gorse darkens the yellow cliff-edge,
And scarlet-flowered trees lean out to drop
Their shadows on the bay below, searching

The water for an image always broken
Between the inward and returning swells.
Farther, beyond the rocks, cuffed by pert waves

Launches tug at their moorings; and in the channel
Yachts that sprint elegantly down the breeze
And earnest liners driving for the north.

Finally, holding all eyes, the long-limbed mountain
Dark on the waves, sunk in a stone composure;
From each far cape the easy flanks lift

In slow unison, purposeful all their rising length,
To meet and lock together faultlessly,
Clasping the notched, worn crater-cone between them.

That cup of fire, drooped like an ageing head,
Is fed with dew now and a paler brightness;
For the rushing anger sank down ages past,

Sank far beneath the sea-bed, leaving only
A useless throat that time gradually stopped
And sealed at last with smoky lichen-skin.

But the mountain still lives out that fiercer life
Beneath its husk of darkness; blind to the age
Scuttling by it over shiftless waters,

The cold beams that wake upon its headlands
To usher night-dazed ships. For it belongs to
A world of fire before the rocks and waters.

CHARLES BRASCH

On Mt. Iron

Red sun, remember
The waterless hills,
Glare of light in
The water-courses.

No milk of cloud
Shall be offered you
From these dried breasts,
To your bronze heaven
No pitying tears.

Thin-skinned the mountains,
And the rocks stained
With crepuscular lichen;
No sap in the thorn,
No voice among shadows.

Red sun, remember
The earth lost in
A shudder of heat.

CHARLES BRASCH

Henley on Taieri

Sullen, the stream gives no clear image back
To the black swan,
Scarcely answers the even, rippling wind
Or press of cloud, but slides
Noiseless in umber coils, eluding
The light that patters on the willow leaves
And flares from the white flanks of the hotel.
Friendless river,
Furtive, scentless,
From gorge to gorge over the yielding plain
Thirstily thrusting;
Saying no word to
Manuka or briar rose
Green bough or golden,
But sidelong, alien,
Onward swirled
Beyond leaves and faces,
No duct of life but
Cold seeker
Of self-dissolution
In the bitter and formless
Light-engulfing
Pit of the desolate sea.

CHARLES BRASCH

The Discovery
(*from Genesis*)

And the sea parted before and closed again behind,
And light and darkness, darkness and light received them.
Beyond the last legendary reef
They swung into ageless calms where the water burned,
Into nights of wild dew struck from shifting stars;
Through currents where leaf or feather drifted
And by the musical archipelagos,
Beaches that sighed for them and green
Tenderness of the palm;
Where black winds wrecked the hideous sea
Lost that cool star on which the heavens turn
And the immortal order of the night
Under whose dispensation the race of man had risen;
And passed on, into a solitary darkness
That hid them each from each in their own confinement
Watching, afraid to sleep; and watching
Slept, and waking found the wind beside them
Dead on a grey mask of water;
Thence for many days and nights
Between the past and future lay,
Hunted by fear and thirst and a swollen sun
And false uncharted stars;
Sighted islands of cloud that promised and deceived
—Strains of song in the wind, imagined birds—
And saw their dawns of promise break
Empty on the sea, and the days falling
Nameless into night
Where cold winds wept with them from a harsher season.

And hope sickened into resignation, signs
No longer promised;
Till one dawn in the endless unfolding of days,
Out of the flights of changing cloud
One cloud grew, keeping place,
Quietly like a seabird settled
And drifted towards them and was land.

CHARLES BRASCH

Poland, October
(*from Nineteen Thirty-nine*)

Even for the defeated life goes on,
Although the codes, assumptions, purposes
That guided and protected them are gone:
They have become the prey of nothingness.

All that was and was known now only seems,
All seeming changes and all change appals,
As they live out the intolerable dreams
That usurp nature to itself grown false.

They have been used and are not wanted any more,
Not by man; they will not be pitied nor
Remembered. Only to suffer are they still free.
Pain can practise new experiments on them,
Until the fair-spoken world their lives condemn
Dies in each one's death. They are history.

CHARLES BRASCH

In Memory of Robin Hyde, 1906–39

He could not win you easily, your death,
Though always hovering near.
Two wars he took for instrument, and that last
Cup of frustration; then he closed and struck
In the sour attic above the summer square,
And you were his and glad to be possessed.

In houses by the sea, through wounded China,
You tempted him defiantly.
Sometimes in conversation we could feel him
Near you, no enemy then, for you would turn,
As though asking for aid, to catch his eye
And hold him in obedience to your will.

By choice you stood always on disputed ground,
At the utmost edge of life,
Gazing into the firepit of disintegration
Whose lavas threaten our small inherited fields,
Whose poisoned fumes and ash of disbelief
Unnerve the quick blood and becloud our vision.

And there about you disease, hysteria, despair
Gathered their monstrous forces,
Corrupting our paper strength, that freely drained
From all we longed for still and still affirmed;
Yet you would not turn away to happiness
In distance and memory where life can be refined.

So they destroyed you. They were stronger. They
   triumph,
Commanding, unmanning us now.
It is their year; harvests of the hapless fall
Before them in Europe, as Gertler here, and Toller
Overtaken at Central Park. Nor shall we know
If those who follow us can put down their rule.

You were an adversary they had to master:
We shall see none to confound them
With blacker courage. Nor shall it be for blame
To have fallen to their power. Only the mightiest
Can really destroy, the darkness they command
Is utter, and their kiss a final calm.

London, December 1939

CHARLES BRASCH

'I Think of Your Generation'

I think of your generation as the youngest
That has found itself, has seen its way in the shadows
Of this despairing age, this country indifferent
To all but the common round, hostile to every
Personal light men would live by. You may not be many,
You that have groped through the stifling dust of existence
And found water—you, shall I say, of the promise,
Scattered, one here and one there, the length of these islands;
To yourselves fumbling, fallible, often bewildered,
Oftener discouraged, your lives strewn with disorder,
And weak, and alone; yet to me as to others the lanterns
We look to, certain stars in a cloudy twilight,
More precious because of your weakness, because you stand
   single.

172

I count with you chiefly that painter, contracted to pity,
Who first laid bare in its offended harshness
The act of our life in this land, expressed the perpetual
Crucifixion of man by man that each must answer,
Rendered in naked light the land's nakedness
That no one before had seen or seeing dared to
Publish—an outrage to all whose comfort trembles
Hollow against such vision of light upon darkness.
And he who meditates under the green escarpments
That bound Wanganui, out of his rank rough acres
Constructing a garden, not in retreat, not escaping
The time's turmoil, but better to focus in quiet
The shrunken image of man; intangible labour
With no clear issue, that yet for a whole generation
May serve to cleanse and sweeten the muddied life-stream
Of trivial daily existence. They too who are planting
Deep in desert Otago Athenian olive,
Virgilian vine, pledges perhaps of a future
Milder and sweeter to mellow blunt hard natures
Of farmer and rabbiter, driver, storekeeper, orchardman,
With usage of wine and oil from grove and vineyard
Shading stony terraces, naked gorges,
Scourged now by frost and fire, no human country.
And that forced listener to the virgin-moded
Tongues of these airy latitudes—grave or smiling
He listens, watchful, bow-strung to attention
Between our human talk and that world-tremor,
Half heard, he conjures into rites of music.
Others will follow; already you can hear them
Rousing, beginning, lighter because they venture
Where some have gone before and marked boldly
A possible way—for you still doubtfully possible,
Demanding all you possess of calm and courage

And edged intellect, and that warmth of spirit
Rarer than beauty—like genius a gift and equivocal.

CHARLES BRASCH

'Waking by Night'
(*from* The Estate)

Waking by night as often I lie in stillness
And feel the hollow dark listening, troubled
As though some far-off note of dread possessed it;
And straining, holding my breath in the suddenly fearful
House, at length half hear, half feel continuous
The fall of winter seas assaulting, racking
This rooted earth and us.

                      Not longest summers
Can end the icy vigil of those waters
Circling the thunderous poles, or still their anguish,
That like a frost striking the helpless midnight
Steals upon earth. So all night through till morning
I hear that fathomless ocean breaking about us
In sleep, and all things borne to dissolution.

J. R. HERVEY

Two Old Men Look at the Sea

They do not speak but into their empty mood
   Receive the leaden utterance of waves,
   And intimations blowing from old graves,
   Men who have already crossed to the torpid sandspit

Between life and death, whose cold rejected hands
Have flung farewell to passion, the brassy lands
Of love and pursuit, who even taste not life
In the pomp of passing synopsis, but only savour
The salty wind and sand swirling up to claim
The total mystery masking in a name.

How shall we live and hold, how love and handle
To the last beach the dark and difficult gleanings?
For so must we come, hugging our recompense,
To the unfeeling shore, to the bleak admonitory tide,
Our fear being as a hand that cups a candle
Against the winds that whiff away pretence,
And the sea whose sentence strikes like a leaden wave.

J. R. HERVEY

Carnival

The day like a respectable woman went
Through the western gate, and the candid eye removed
Let in the tribes of folly; and desire
Reddened the streets, and even wisdom put by
The tripping cloak, and the watcher in the tower
Rejected the stars when song came reaching up.

And the children leaving their cold and sterile sleep
At the hungry windows were stained with carnival:
Confetti sprayed them like seed whose burning bloom
Should war upon the white integrities.

Music no longer monkish paced the heart,
Hooded with admonition; but now, in the antic
And shameless motley, yellowed the aloof temple
With reckless cymbals and gauds of holiday:
Nor did the drums revive the shining battle,
But dashed their proud raptures upon the clowning stage.

The lips frozen by vow were loosed; the women
Preferring not love, where, isled in a surge of lovers,
Her teasing beauty knew its appointed hour:
How should she walk the black and whispering lane,
Chosen of light, swung in the pampered car?

Pleasure was rotten-ripe, whose juice restored
Old men to the sappy dream; and young men staggered
Beneath the mounting fevers; and the comely cobbles
Of the frugal market-going feet were fired
With the dancing fame, and houses that received
Austere, weathered, each day a sunset glance,
Knew on their face a guilty blandishment.

And the night dragged its long red length until
The torches flickered, and returning shadows blew
On the scattered laughs, and coldly the season
Sat on spreadeagled flesh while death the rag-picker
Fingered the frolic bones beneath the clock.

J. R. HERVEY

Man of Crete

I, Brotachus of Gortyna, a Cretan, lie here, not having come hither for this, but for traffic.—An ancient epitaph in Greece.

I, Brotachus, came not hither
That I might barter blood and passion
For death's disabling fashion.

I was no huckster, crying
Muscle and mighty look that death,
Catching a bargain in my breath,
Should accept and set me lying.

Was it possible that out of the white room
Of Crete walking I should fumble
At the door so adequate, see crumble
My last design, sing down the street of doom?

My eyes and fingers loved
As a woman the waters caring
For my merchandise, bearing
My desire to the principality
Where wonders moved.

But I came for traffic, expecting
The assemblage of tongues, the hungry palms:
Not the decree of silence,
Not, crashing down, the constricting arms.

Brotachus, once of Gortyna,
Now of the tomb, ask for me never:
For here is my name fastened, frozen forever
My homely artifice,
I came not for this.

J. R. HERVEY

Threnos

Each day sees die the lonely leaf, sees die
The perfect paw, the unobstructed wing,
 Sees stooping from the arena
 The flesh with death on shoulder.

These are the fringes of disaster announcing
The slow, mesmeric tide, the heedless wash,
 And here my proud ones gather
 The bone, the claw, the feather.

But where the moon of wonder lights the forest,
And love looks out of the window, and the white wing
 Of song relents, no augur
 Hints of the destroyer.

Or so I considered until the emissary,
And now each day sees die the dream, the lover;
 Ah, who will stand forever,
 Out of this coil deliver?

J. R. HERVEY

Neighbour

He is a hat and coat
Disappearing through the abrupt gate
That delivers him from
The scald of scrutiny.

He is my neighbour, further
From my knowledge than those
At the world's edge of whom
The record flows.

I cannot follow him where he
Goes through mute corridors and where
His desires are known to himself,
And shines his unshared ecstasy.

His pilgrimage through the dark house
Is over mountains, he is broken,
But the fence is final, not to me
The news is spoken.

J. R. HERVEY

John Donne's Defiance

(*John Donne, poet, formerly libertine, and latterly Dean of St. Paul's—1621—a short time before his death commissioned a portrait of himself in which he was to be represented standing upon an urn and wrapped in his own burial shroud.*)

Now is the hour of the bell, now am I caught
Out of the war whose sullen stain I wear:
Yet must I first oppose the final malice
Of death to whom my wall's a window inviting
His freezing stare on my enfeeblement.

My enemy has been a cloud confronting
The sun, has been a snake whose poison glittered
Over the environs of love, for in the midst
Of ecstasy even has this dismal horn
Usurped the hour, so that my sweets dissolved,
Turning to bitter the leniency of love.

The sensual night in which my joys appeared
As stars was still the night, and this life heavy
With satisfactions was but death dispensing
The sly draught of destruction. My song was fed,
No less than my desire, with casual loves,
But when these blew away like petals, remained
Oracular death loading the time with judgment.

I would not be taken by death in sleep, nor snatched
Out of an idle temper, but he must win
My body in battle, outwit the constant will:
Yet is the victory mine for every blow
But makes that prison to perish wherein the King,
My soul, awaits the august deliverance.

This room that reeks corruption, here have I laid
My strength away but not athletic hope,
And I have drawn the curtains of repentance,
So that no loves may pry and pierce with guilt
The man now altogether bled of passion.

Christ, my Anchor, will hold this ship against
The urgent tide, and out of this lane of sorrow
Will God the Father bring me to broad estate:
Therefore I summon death that he may see
The front of my faith, and know that the bell tolls
For him out of this clear and calm event.

Bring then the urn that prates of dust and I
Will stand upon it, setting my foot on fear,
And trampling stern pretences of the grave,
For He enables this boldness Whose feet were iron
On the snake's head, the tempter, sliming the ages.

Now lightly on arm I bear my heavy shroud
That ye may bind my body affixing knots
At head and foot like locks that cry forbiddance
To thought and life's decorous liberty:
But let my face be seen that its defiance
May arm the trembler dreaming dissolution.

So do I make an end, my portrait shall be
A scorn of symbols advertising doom—
What a death is this life, and what a resurrection
This death, this fitful dark declaring light.

J. R. HERVEY

Hydro Works

First the valley where the houses
Are cherished by hedges and trees,
The pastures flowing green
To the river, the willows
Frail against a face of rock.
Nothing to threaten the eye,
Sheep penned in the peace of summer,
Larks with the song of certitude.

Emerging from the valley the mind
Encounters like an enemy, itself,
Rock-like in the cowering wilderness:
The idling spirit
Recoils from the resolute wall,
The squat citadel spraying power.

And the hills stand in submission
And the dumb, disciplined waters;
For harder than driven stone or defiant rock
The hard core of the purpose and will of man.

J. R. HERVEY

The Man Who Wanted to be a Seagull

He chose the sea, mother, emancipator,
(Spendthrift of seamen's hopes, cloaking a knell)
Attained the sea-blue heart and salted speech,
And the cruising bird's intent exploratory eye.

Especially his perennial longing reached
Out to the gull and its immaculate freedom:
He loved them even when, desultory in harbours,
Their lust probed the slack and dubious waters.

No saintly rapture after his body's shipwreck,
But he would look forward and through his death and see
Himself as a gull in smoothest searching flight,
Between the sea and sky his wandering heaven.

And when at last he felt the fatal wind
He smiled, expecting wings of liberty.

J. R. HERVEY

Sonnet of Departure

The room of peering shadows holds her fast:
   Deep is the pit from which she would not rise:
   Her spirit is upon some enterprise
In a far field where all her dreams are cast:
A world weighs on her lids, this being past,
   And all its legend gathered from her eyes,
   So that it is the dizzy world that dies
Like a mad wheel whose motion cannot last.

Here lie the littered years, the fading heart,
The fettered love whose every word is spoken:
This is the night and turning where we part,
For one by one the living links are broken,
   And, mingled in the ceremony of death,
   Love and the silence watch a hastening breath.

Shunting

These trucks and coaches, only yesterday,
Rolled through home counties, mile on metal mile;
Some with smooth speed, their open eyes of glass
Pupilled with passengers, while others went
Jolting along with homely jobs to do
From town to town. Now all alike assemble
Like branded sheep in this impartial yard,
Where they are rounded up with clank and puff,
And driven with efficient fuss of steam.
The whistling engine moves an inch, and sends
Concussions jumping down the coupled line;
Men wash the coaches clean with dripping mops,
Or step with peril among treacherous rails
To shift the levers which will organise,
Sort, and divide these trains that will be seen
Going on peaceful errands through green shires
With splendid salutations of white smoke.

BASIL DOWLING

Mortal Love

How frail is mortal love
    With nought to oppose it:
The ghost of a word or a whim
    Quite overthrows it.

But see, when sorrow and pain
    Stand up to prove it,
Not they with their batteries,
    Nor death, can move it.

BASIL DOWLING

Naseby: Late Autumn

Larches about this retrospective town
Display their gold not laboured at nor spun.
But in this man-made chasm, yellow-brown,
A wiry miner elbow-numb with cold
Gumbooted stands and with his swivel gun
Boils down whole hillsides for a different gold
More loved than autumn larch, gorse bloom, or sun.
Fierce water with incessant soft explosion
Bores and devours and sifts rich clay from stone,
Divorcing with its terrible erosion
The body of earth from fundamental bone.

Sly gold eludes my fumblings with a dish
Until experience, with tilt and swish,
Cradles and coaxes out each shiny flake.
So satisfied I stumble down the slope
By mustard creek and small sky-gazing lake
Musing on man and mineral, and take
This gleam of greed home in an envelope.

BASIL DOWLING

Summer Afternoon

Through drowsy stillness drifts a sound of mowing.
A crested quail from the hedge-top is crowing.
A cricket sets his midget motor going.

Over the hill white clouds in prosperous masses
Shepherd their shadows on the sunburnt grasses
While summer day to summer evening passes.

BASIL DOWLING

The Air in Spring

Where leaves are glassy green
On this spring morning as though submarine,
And apple blossom white
Blushes as coral to a diver's sight,
Out of my depth am I
In this clear stream whose surface is the sky.

While waving treetop shows
Which way the light invisible current flows,
And grasses bending over
Tell how it leans upon them like a lover,
I let my palate savour
Sweet air that like fresh water has no flavour.

Small birds, bright fishes, swim
And dart among the branches cool and dim,
And overhead that hawk
Hovering in blue distance is a shark:
We all would only drown
If we broke surface more than staying down.

BASIL DOWLING

Canterbury

On this great plain the eye
Sees less of land than sky,
And men seem to inhabit here
As much the cloud-crossed hemisphere
As the flat earth. Trains travel fast and straight,
And travellers early or late
Think of their destination
More than of pasture, wheatfield, wayside station.
Here birds and winds fly free,
And tree is miles from tree
Except where in dark ranks they muster
Against the gales or cluster
Befriending lonely farms.
Tired tramps and trampers fare
Sadly along the endless roads, but the hare
Is lucky, and the magpie, black and white
Highwayman with his shout.
Sounds are soon dead being echoless
In the vast emptiness,
Though thunder and the ocean roar
Carry, on calm days, far:

And some sounds hardly ever rest:
The sound of wind from nor'east or nor'west
And three great rivers with proud Maori names
Chafing worn shingle till the ocean tames
Their wildness. This is my holy land
Of childhood. Trying to comprehend
And learn it like the features of a friend,
Sight rides on power-poles and tops of trees
From the long eastern beaches and loud seas
League after league
Till definition fades in bluish vague
Distance: then dreams begin
To see in vision colourless and thin
Beyond the western foothills lost
The huge and desolate ranges of the Coast.

BASIL DOWLING

Walking in Bush

Resisted by the tangle
Of this strange temperate jungle
I tread on felt of mosses and tiny ferns
While a neat fantail with his needle note
Lighter than air and black as soot
Tosses about me. Day to twilight turns,
And drowned are colours to a dim marine
Mingling of brown and green;
Except where, high up in a gap,
That towering rimu wears a crimson cape
Of rata bloom. No wild beasts here
But small bright eyes of berries peer,

Armed lawyer holds me back
And fangless serpent of looped supplejack.
Odour of mould envelops all
With messages of death, yet life
Is riotous and rife.
Trees live on where they fall
And in decay immortal grown
Flourish with new foliage not their own.
On branches without leaves
Lichen its grey beard weaves
And busy creeper fits loose-knitted sleeves.
All is wet stillness and fertility.

This might be Eden and that bird
The same that Eve and Adam heard
Chime in their green-aisled paradise
Before the coiled destroyer's lies
Whispered. As I emerge from shade
I meet the sunlight flashing like a blade.

BASIL DOWLING

The Early Days

Comforts were few in eighteen-fifty-five,
They got up at dawn and they had to strive
With element and enemy to keep alive
And were lucky if they lived to woo and wive
    In the early, early days.

O joy was a stubborn and costly boon
To those young lovers on their honeymoon:
They met a flooded river as night came on
And horses and riders were all swept down
    In the early, early days.

189

We're all sane, but there were madmen then
Like old Sir Thomas Tancred who fired his gun
Through a drawing-room window at a prowling man
That was only a sunflower looking in
    In the early, early days.

One captain at sea drank more than he ought
And set his course for the rocks, but they caught
And drugged him though he cursed and fought,
So the ship came safe to Lyttelton port
    In the early, early days.

I've read of a serving Australian black
Who would run from Mount Peel to Ashburton and back
And want no wages but a glass of sack.
Poor fellow, he died with a rope round his neck
    In the early, early days.

And where is the equal of Parson Gore
Who pausing once in his sermon swore
He heard a wild pig go past the door
And the whole congregation ran to hunt the boar
    In the early, early days.

The sun was fiercer then on plain and steep,
The rain fell heavier, the snow more deep,
And a house in the wind was a rocking ship.
Now the folk it buffeted are all asleep
    In the early, early days.

History tells us they were hard and bold;
They carved out forests and they dug for gold,
But many died young and some died old
And their passionate hearts are quiet and cold
    In the early, early days.

ANTON VOGT

from For England, in Grateful Appreciation

I

I was five when we moved to England, and the strange voices
Were more marvellous than wax-works;
And the elevator boy in the big hotel made us laugh,
Noisily, like foreigners.

We had a house later, on the River.
It cost 13 guineas a week, and there were staircases
And rooms for the maids, and highflown people week-ended
And ate kippers or bacon and eggs and played billiards.

Money came easily in the boom, and the *nouveau riche*
Were not all ill-bred or British.

The lawn sloped to a private canal shared by sixteen houses.
England was croquet and roses and speckled carp
Caught on a bent pin and served for breakfast.

Our boat had blue cushions, and the men wore flannels;
And the balloons were a barrage of colour in a bright sky.
Summer was strangely long in retrospect.

On regatta days the punts gathered by the green islands
Where the gramophone played;
We threw crumbs to the ducks, and fished for minnows,
And watched the thick crusts course down the long necks
Of the tame swans . . .

We went to the City occasionally, but not often.
We travelled in tubes and were good and didn't touch.
We saw Charlie Chaplin and Mary Pickford, and sometimes
even a Guardsman
Stiff like a toy under a magnifying glass.

On a fine day in crowds we saw Princess Mary,
But I remember best an old lady selling corsets;
They were lovely and pink and full of gadgets
And they cost nineteen shillings elevenpence three-farthings
Which was very English.

We visited obscure relations of the Cook General in the East
End,
And were introduced as the young sir and the little lady;
And the periwinkles and cucumber sandwiches
Were more terrifying than frogslegs.

But the most remarkable thing about England,
Was that the bread was white.

ANTON VOGT

For a Child's Drawing

This death-mask is my portrait by my son,
Whose childish eyes can trace the years' deep lines
Naively innocent of all they mean,
Shaping in shade what I had thought concealed.

Deftly his fingers find the flagging chin,
And fondly press the parted lips quite shut,
As if he feared that foolish words might spring
Prehensile from the hunger of my heart.

So with light hand he sketches what his mind
Has learned to love, and therefore can forgive;
Shows me myself, in being me to him,
Who cannot know me as I really am.

Then closes the eyes that dare no longer see
Save hooded, their erratic destiny.

HUBERT WITHEFORD

Elegy in the Orongorongo Valley

Sundered from this beauty is its fond lover
Who wandered in boredom over far oceans
Again and again remembering, till the day
When decks split in flame and the sea choked him.

Did his despairing salt-water stormed eye-balls
Search, as they broke, for these streams sprawling
Over high places, the mountains of springtime,
Out of the world on a lost morning?

Did death's lightning show him this shadowed valley
Burning through oceans, green beyond time?
Was this the river he felt closing over
Islands of pain and over his life?

Here and in exile and in last anguish
He found no frenzy to win him this wanton—
In his full failure glistens the wild bush
Too long remembered, too long forgotten.

HUBERT WITHEFORD

The Magnolia Tree

Forth from earth's opened side
The slow, slow fountain plays,
Its twisted streams of wood
Flowing to the measure of a giant time
To statelier music than our lives may know.

And on their currents' crest
Green leaves, white petals foam
Through whose fragility
The rapid pulse of spring
Beats with a fairer and more fatal stroke
Than, in our veins, its keenest rage achieved.

HUBERT WITHEFORD

Invasion

Tumultuously move against my heart
Fresh images of armies wrecked on death

And reddened waves' dark ecstasy defiles
The basalt walls that guard its quietness

The archer on the highest tower looks downwards
Upon an earth no longer free from wrath

His golden armour clashes as he strikes
Gauntleted fist upon the swinging gong

194

Through all the castle he sets light to fear
And every window glistens into life

Halls that were silent such long time before
Are wakened as the men-at-arms rush by

Then lightning's shock has faded and all know
Water and blood are powerless against stone

And all the night in natural jubilee
Over a sea of blood rings the heart's revelry.

HUBERT WITHEFORD

Alone

The silence still and no sun burns above
And this the ninth day on the promised coast
To which through many griefs I came
Past blackened cities and calm fields of death.
This is the trysting place, its certain signs—
The congealed sea, the bones of ancient fire
And in the ruined cliffs a shallow cave.

Upon the frozen sands only my steps
Send their clear echoes forth to die alone.
The corrupt cliffs have fallen and are still;
The ice is thick above the avalanche.
Past is the time when, from the dying sea,
The flabby dolphins threshed upon the beach,
The last great tendrils unclasped from the rock.

Beneath the unchanging sky nine days have passed
And I begin to see the dark ring close
And guess the manner of your coming here.
For now no more in terror nor in hope
I stare at the few blackened sticks without,
Kindled long since to be my whole world's ash.
I yield before the silence and I know
Your servants who are waiting at my side.

HUBERT WITHEFORD

At the Discharge of Cannon Rise the Drowned

The morning that he drowned the white ship came,
It anchored in the waters where he lay.

Some days then, by our time, of windless rain
That poured and ebbed to shroud or almost show
The unpeopled decks, the looming guardian
On the phantasmal world where no clock marks
Duration of the cold abandonments
And weird acceptances that lead man hence.

But from the flickering scene one stark vignette
Glares in ambiguous hues of hope and death—
Out of the port-hole bursts a smear of flame,
A blast of thunder from the flood rebounds
With gliding leap, impelled by answering fire,
Lazarus rises from his restless couch.

Now his corrupted life is as the charge
Exploded in the cannon's narrow depth,
Native no longer of the earth he springs
Breaking the waters he surrendered in
And as he leaves the limbo of vague dream
Out of the wash and weed he plucks his death.

So back from harbour to a mounting storm,
Into the gale that blows from their high port
Back from mortality the huge sails slide.

KENDRICK SMITHYMAN

Walk Past Those Houses on a Sunday Morning

Walk past those houses on a Sunday morning
with a piano stumbling in the front room,
where the mechanic freed from tools takes shears
to clip his hedges, talk of politics.

Or move along the lake, or down the track
sit under butts of logs and watch the mangroves,
the chips, the pottery shards; there distant farms
grow out of fog to sun; for it was here
that pedant summer rose to teach us fate.

Think how the threads were coming close together:
remember the month, the day, the hour, and the
ungainly kitbag dragged off home in the tram and two days
    after
set in the hot Waikato close to the river—
bell tents, new straw, and uniforms everywhere.

Leave was a chance to take the bike
and go crawling into the ranges. Here were places
not to be seen as before, and places to visit:
a house with oaks where there was one
was quick with sympathy but did not understand.

Remember all these things: the League ball punted across the
    park
processional the sails of eighteen footers
and a cold salad at five.

Somewhere there is value to them. As the piano stumbles
something grows into being. It will take shape in the end.

KENDRICK SMITHYMAN

This Blonde Girl

This blonde girl carries sorrow on her shoulder
and all my world swings at her fingertips
darkness and light, while red as a berry her lips
make marks of music on me that never colder
the legendary spheres may equal. She will sing
through every ocean chapel of my being
and bird be of my eye at waking morning,
perched on the twig of a time will never stop.

And if I come to her it is to tell
how she inhabits me and moves like water
through these intrinsic habits and may rove
freelance of my whole image now and later,
having walked innocent in wonder and in all
of harm familiar, grown up again to love.

KENDRICK SMITHYMAN

from Considerations of Norfolk Island

I

High in the afternoon the dove
winds melancholy to his mate
a thread of music, monotone
upon the languid afternoon
the language of his simple love,
his phrases breaking through the heat.

Heraldic and primeval birds
reflect from their neglected tree
the clemency we did not know,
the charity we could not say,
who kept behind our uncouth words
a terrifying privacy.

Returned to memory they wind
now simply out notc undcr notc
our pain commingled with their song,
the pain of music that must hang
like heat stiff on the lazy wind
and stab our history to the heart.

KENDRICK SMITHYMAN

Icarus

Now on the shining
back breaking water
while the lucid
bird in his high tree
sings and the ploughman
opens the hillside
it is no matter
that a boy should fall
no planet, human
entering the water.

And ships in furrows
and fields in their waves
neither a bird
nor a boy attend
and the proper grief of
his father who watches
a while may be heard
till the song, the sorrow,
are lost on the waves.

KENDRICK SMITHYMAN

The Moment

But, breaking day, their several flutes
the birds uplifting in the park,
paying a ravelled thread from note to note,
entwine the meanings which their songs

might be, as though their threads so met
(sound across sound) to hold at centre
a space, a silence otherwise then to be,
communication's analogue of me,
who draw towards that core, that sphere,
to be informed upon the empty zone.
And one detached, one thread alone may lead
between the intricate avenues of trees
to where he waits, a god of silence.
He, Hermes, the power of embassy,
dawn colour of copper, blue-robed,
whom I meet above the tired waterway,
beyond the branches of the olive trees.

By day the workmen's gnarled fingers are
like olive branches, or spread as roots
to enter the soil I am, to trap and tap
and drain.
            I catch hints of the god's presence
from the corner of the eye, in windows
turning towards a shadow. A flash of blue,
a gleam of copper. And, always, it is a dress
someone wears without distinction, or a bowl
another puts aside for cleaning. Are these
his intimations that he comes in his own time,
his time may not be mine, or yours, or ours?
I cannot think how we may enter with him,
but suspect his empty zone has richness
we may not find daily surrounding ourselves
with possessing and wanting. His abnegation
is perhaps truer than our sore affirmations,
perhaps his silence all our words enclose.

It is then as though all were sealed,
firmly.

        A vacant crystal space
forbidding sound; as a silent field
in summer, foreshadowing ripeness,
may not speak.

             Yet, seeming to enter,
and wishful then wholly to surrender,
our every device and all defence.

It is then sits behind the known face
the unknown bone and the spirit therein,
foreshadowed ripeness in our silence
to be reaped at speaking.

             There is, alas,
no word for that moment, we may not
ever find a word.

             None is revealed.

KENDRICK SMITHYMAN

Waiwera

Dozing on sand we make our fresh resolutions,
secured to our indecisions, within reach of
Gulf murmur, cicada song quickly, quickly stitching
this afternoon (not otherwise to be) to us.
The bay is called Waiwera.

Now beating back and forth the kahawai birds
work from the wharf to the rocks, channel threading
and swinging and settling and rising, sometimes
checking as though to ask *Why?* A school of fish
answers them. Then sprats whirl, the terns strike.

A soldier turns his face to the ringing summer
as a flower twists painfully, or with a puzzling
regard most like a blind child's. Inland, thunder-
heads form. Our fine day is being dismantled.
The cricket teams are moving off to their cars.

Gulf murmur, cicada song turned under a thrust
thumb-and-forefinger of tree roots, from a scar
where earth fell off the tilted strata. Tree
hung over the boulders and us, other injunction
made to a mood to wag on another word.

They are all secure. The emblems and the images
are in temper and context. Take them as you will
here we belong, here we bring our kids and lunches
grief and guilt and game as Sunday travellers
not to feel out of place, ourselves to enjoy.

Does a worm mumble heartwood of the Norfolk pine?
Or the marram for nothing strand like a star upon
drift branch and fence line? The warm spring
idiotically bubble away? Is there more meaning
than made by the wind chasing the tide around?

Puzzled, the soldier is at home. His gaze enquires
warrant of manuka slope for his content to abide
so in reach of breeze, Gulf murmur, cicada song,
to wear his brutality as a child its blindness.
To the custom of such a world he offers himself.

KENDRICK SMITHYMAN

Could You Once Regain

Girl, could you once regain
that pitiless mask!
                 It is drawn
through the flesh's suffering
from your inmost tranquil bone,
when, shaken by love you lie
purged of the weights of a day,
your face unbelievably pure
as though bone lit with clarity,
transparency fired by the act
of love to possess your feature
and sharpen out of its firing
some other disguised nature.

If you held that purity
of your body, then, in repose,
where knowledge had seemed to be
self-knowing, self-aware—
                 I propose
a chaos. For should you go out
in the bitter livid street,
the young would be disgraced, bent
men be momently straight,
the huddled world raise a shout
for the face not seen since the day
when a wall and a city went down
and the Trojan suffered the clown
to stare on her pride.

I pray

again to be snared by that light
floods from your face when love
has shaken us through and world
is most perfectly perceived
by the afterglow, as the light
dies back to the tranquil bone,
and, commingling, we may stretch
and companionably yawn,
resuming the suffering flesh
by which we are daily grieved.

KENDRICK SMITHYMAN

Dirge for Two Clavichords and Bowler Hat

All day that metronome, thrice gallant heart,
ails of its musing but declines to stay.
Now between rounds of gin in city bars
some tell, but softly, how Troy had its day
and fell caught in its musing on delay, delay
which echoes with the echoing barman's voice
while at the doorstep dogs lie down and moan
and Waring cries, 'Why! Have I now no choice?'
as each one leaves and he is left alone.

Come, let us call upon Count Ivanhoe
that innocent of enthusiastic flesh
who's free of vulgar and of obvious vice,
—unless that scent is meths upon his breath—
and with him pass in song a certain time
until, responsive to his sad metronome,
one sits aside deliberating his death
and calls for taxis, wearying for his home.

205

Should I sit down, or at the other door
look out for pardon or look in for sin,
Troy falling round my shoulders as a whore
discards a brassiere in the rubbish tin?
Speak, Ivanhoe. Waring, say what you think.
One sleeps, and one flicks ashes in his drink.

'Your foot from brothels!' Hear the Ancient shriek
who does not feel how wind is drawing south
or know too soon too late he will be weak
to thrust the clay-bone fingers off his mouth.
Those bachelors of reverence, the dead
ride out of origin against the host.
I find a mouse turd in my latest bread
(a frantic gull hurtles the wild sour coast)
and bitter song breaks, breaks, in Waring's head.

This country has no moles—there's pity there,
and by such lack our generation's wronged
or something flicks last lustre in our thought.
I hear a stylish master *blind mole casts*
Copp'd hills towards heaven, to tell the earth is throng'd
By man's oppression; and the poor worm doth die for 't.
Waring's for worms. His whisky will squat long
waiting his kiss across the glass's brim,
and Ivanhoe, and each clapped and cursèd whore,
and all who fumble at the great rubbish bin.

The hounds of doorways think this no great matter.

KENDRICK SMITHYMAN

Personal Poem

Dearest my wife who lies
evenings alone with sickness
husbanding, consuming her year.
She whose time flags and flies
I have no power for, nor bear
a miracle word into her weakness
to startle and make clear her eyes;
but sit alone, apart from her
devising histories of my regard.

What power lies in what was shared
and then known good? None, none,
and the glass of profit, cracked,
miserably looks back. The undone
day is not revoked but yet undone
surrenders all we cared,
that we, fantastically loving,
swore would never slip away.
           She stirred
once, falling sleepy from caress,
as snipe cried passing on above
harbour and park and street and house,
murmuring with a desperate voice
against the night, *My loss, my loss*
and slept, small prophet of duress
while sadly I lay powerless, less.

KENDRICK SMITHYMAN

Evening Music

The flute begins to falter, to fidget, to fret.
He puts it by, and smokes while evening clouds
with rain which will not fall through four months
of unremitted drought, and his carnations die.

His grief, his mourning, cannot speak to him
in picture or book, but only through his flute
does he allow himself to talk of something going
always away before his hand might have possessed,
before the love he has not offered answered
another love as the harmonics answer his notes.

Phrase out of phrase, their hesitating passion
sings expressionless from clumsy breath and finger.
In pine shadow, evening shadow, he essays piping
thin shadow of song out of date

> *I wish in the*
gloaming in the valley of the moon of despair
I had someone Who someone one to love me Who
my darling O my darling

in the thin evening, see,
he leans on doorsill, braces dangling, dragging
so very sad his eyes from little boys and girls.

KENDRICK SMITHYMAN

The Night Walkers

Why should those birds disturb us as they walk
the dark fronds of the sea at half or at low tide,
those red-legged stilts and small godwit, pied
alike by the moon, at their melancholy work?
In all the calm and plenty of moonlight they take
sudden excited flight until need to dance has died
from the air, then settling again, restive, stride
between sand and sea till tide rise or morning break.

They are doing no more than picking out their food
and yet they pause to cry or wheel, and their cries
weep through the night to us who cannot understand.
What reason shakes to mourning in them who land
and sea frequent, who simple from their food must rise
warning no calm is without pain and death upon the flood?

KENDRICK SMITHYMAN

Elegy Against a Latter Day
A. L. S., 1879–1945

I

As though he could hold all in consciousness,
all meaning and all purpose of his life and world,
hold all in infinitely suffering apprehension,
I imagined a man this night whose thought fastened
quick on a seven-branched candelabra until each flame
stood individually; and then all changed, each became

a great golden and hierarchic cross, but yet no cross
out of Christian myth or of a Christian condition
but solely image. His power was in upholding tension
and in excluding. Only so might that talent be uncurled
from the accretions of his daily life, from the distress
of being and its crowd. Then, perhaps jealous of him,
I dismissed him and destroyed his fiction, his image
fed with dish-water down the drain.

                            Meanwhile, time
which is a sutler's burden as much as king's or statesman's,
set up a hoarse voice in the lamp above me and I furled
tea-towel and oven-cloth, and could not stop to entertain
suffering infinity.

                  But where I had not fixed my thought
another image came persisting, which with it brought
vision of suffering and endurance I imagined had long been
sealed and drained of any strength to make me suffer.
Remembered death three years growing unwilling I had seen
set up before me death and memory of my mother.

II

A certain death dies from us being young. Alone,
waking from walking in sleep you know it is there
and happening to you in the endless dark; in frenzy
of dark and unknowing you, child, feel an outgoing
which is like and is a certain dying, is another
death to die from us who panic and wail in fear
in unknowing dread of darkness that no fancy
will build for you now, when you sob alone in the hall
but cannot tell you will not be the same again
as you were in the moment's shock before you could call.
Did you call, or was it your crying brought a light

and your mother to comfort the wildness of misery,
to solace the lack that was worse than then known pain?
I think of the dark as it seemed in a terrible night
when I woke from sleep in an unknown place, alone,
believing we may not escape from that rigorous history
of childhood and its bewildered sombre unmeaning;
and now I cast an image of death, of dying known
to the dying, act to the actor, since once moaning
a child stood; thinking now—For the dying, is there
a moment when they stand in darkness bewildered, stand
alone as the child I was stood once in midnight calling?
In fear and in need, stand crying?
                              I remember
loss, loss burned through me held to that island
when my mother lay dying, pleading they said, and calling.

III

My god of grief lashed hale to his whipping post,
speak for me, swear for me now, swear in my anthem
all poems I have never dared to write O wear me down
to the bone of a word to tell her out in a poem
debt like a flower springs fine and rises up slowly,
against the everywhere of years endures to thrust
its rose against these winds would steep, would drown
her worth and wound under their blowing dully, daily.

I cannot settle a word for that heavy body bore me
three days labouring who three years bore with snarl
and claw of the crabs of pain, who was like such rock
monsters patrol, who cried against the known churl
of betraying flesh a hospice to her death unwanted,

who had great lasting forceful spirit and much charity
to live by recital of others, and took her own stroke
minute by minute, and lay down, and was still unstunted.

My god, grieve—I cry up the unimportant dead
gone down in a time of war who fought only with their lives
and were to love vulnerable as always to their living;
and cry her among them who, gone down, receives and gives
meaning into my loving another and these two small sons.
Cry when the guilty insufficiencies rage in my head
that not otherwise it seems are we sustained in loving
by terms of grief which her example holds, and pardons.

KENDRICK SMITHYMAN

Defenceless Children, Your Great Enemy

Defenceless children, your great enemy
Has still no face. You cannot take his hand
To hope that he will laugh because your boat
Turns upside down, nor call him pretty names.
Hard, hard to understand
He does not hate or love you.   There are many
Deceive. He will not trick you, shames
Indeed our little habits of deceit,
But will in his own time destroy, work ill,
Pervert, whatever pleases him. *Miserere*,
The clock at night cries upon its shelf,
And *Consummatum est* again it cries.
Perhaps the enemy is just yourself,
Or God, or Fate, or Time, or Vanity,
Or Chance the cacodemon whom none flies.

I cannot tell, I shall not ever know
More than I say, that something works to wrong
The simplest dream and that always they grow
Profitless prophets we had thought most strong
In casting tea-leaves to decide the hour
Or divinate the lucky anodyne.
He gives no sign.
Until his work is over and complete
And ruefully you testify his power.

KENDRICK SMITHYMAN

Incident at Matauri

Shags or, they say, occasional a white
heron print a waste of beach between tides.
Like catchcries fallen from that air bright
brown are surprising seaweeds. There's no wharf
cither way, miles; thread foam trails sand
below day broken on rough grazing, or a land
clipped by sheep. There no calls descend
through speculations down. Only the shell,
weed, tussock, cutty grass, scrub and rub
of the wearing wind serpentines a minute
from what we mean by it, designing bay or bluff.
Space, largely, fills vision and prospect, and could
be barc cxcept seas flow or those islands curl.

Look out then if you go that way by the east
holding your native sense to that nothing
complete in its now estates.
                    A morning took
two, thought them secure, by a small flurry,

(they left their cat sleeping out the fire)
with dawn a sail away from their fished channel.
Took two, with tackle ready, motor going.
Nothing rolled down the pebbles after them.
Space, suppose largely, was before them.

Print by print or at the lost step hemmed
a morning light surprised on those beaches
thread of foam and the motor's distant rocking.
Rocking and distant the islands slept.

JAMES BERTRAM

Rondeau in Wartime

No nearer home than Nassau Bay
Or Marathon or Mandalay
Fly-bitten sons of Britain fight
For God and Empire and the Light
Of Asia, dim at half-a-crown a day.

Far-called our Navies melt away
While padres lift their hands to pray
For squaddies pitching tents each night
No nearer Home.

So leave the Generals still at play
(Crowned by some simple leaf or bay)
These walk by faith and not by sight
And those who died to prove them right
Need ask—content with common clay—
No nearer home.

Epitaph for an American Bomber
Tokyo, March 1945

In this enemy city where your winged danger
brushed night skies in catherine-wheel crescendo
to light these candles these obsequies these tremendous
inorganic pillars of anger

and our hearts hallowed it, tautstrung like antennae
to hope or horror for the B-29 burning
o disastrous nightship drinking white fire and turning
quenched now, in the dark bay.

The song of young fliers drowns in the dirge of Icarus.
But we, on a ruined morning in windy Tokyo,
cannot breathe for the ashes that choke our sorrow
and a grief beyond tears

for what we have seen: these shadow-shapes in file
picking their lost way dazed among dead who are lucky
and may not watch, as we must, a blind man breaking
the rag doll that was a child.

LOUIS JOHNSON
Elegy

Fond, frozen, first and only lover,
Lost are my last, the only words that count;
Brilliant as but an echo of that past
Memory will choose, like words, few scenes from many.

There is a ripple on the face of death,
And I am holding the last strands of reason
In this symbolic grass, with twitching fingers
Plucked from the brown earth, and you are quiet.

Without response, alone, without reprieve;
Unless the wheeling gull comes as a sign,
Unless the resurrection of the flower
Breathes a new myth into the elegy.

LOUIS JOHNSON

Dirge

We built our love up like a work of art,
Increasing and subtracting as we came
First through the birth-world of redoubled Spring
And afterwards through flame.

But when the hell of the attendant smoke
Burst through the chemistry of you and I,
We were the victims of each other's hands
Not knowing how or why.

We consumed love at that first brief encounter,
And having nothing, on each other turned
With hands of hate to tear the other up
To see if love still burned.

LOUIS JOHNSON

Pygmalion

With love he shaped the limbs, her breasts arose
Out of his heart, fastened upon the eye
And brushed his mouth, cupiditous and wild
With supplications that the chill would pass
From stone-cold flesh—that she would glow with life.

And her eye flushed, and breath distilled her throat
Where blood leapt cataracts, finding her voice,
Answering him, making his labour seem
All-wise and beautiful as they lay down
To wreak their love upon each other's bones.

But, in the brassy morning, when his eye
Found the first trace of ravage in her mould,
He knew that she would age and waste away,
The breasts sag, and the joints grow gaunt and rust—
And wished that she again were faultless stone.

LOUIS JOHNSON

Mother of a Daughter

What she fears in her child is what
in love her own loin yielded, shielded the joy
that knew, conceded all the heart
in her day for her own bright boy

who shone in the moon like a sun,
coming by night through silent, trembling seconds
that were her heart counting, her blood
lying open and taut for the word that thickens

to welcome his coming with claiming hands.
Oh, mad her fingers then that took
more than an eye can hold, or heart,
so full that saying, senses, shook

the night. Empty her womb now; hours
hang heavy since his death, and rage
that her knowledge, jealously kept, may turn
to bitter usage on the daughter's page and singe

in that sense of Hell that terrifies—that was
real too, when it happened to her, but not
so keen as blood, as cry of trembling womb
when he came, turning the latch in its socket

locking their secret frenzy to themselves.
'Oh daughter, oh my daughter whom I mourn
under the cinder moon's decrepit eye.'
But foremost fear is of the youth once worn

on her own skin like magic: shrivelled now
with the rancorous pulse of helpless age
that sets a viper's tooth at the door for eunuch,
a totem to curdle love to her own blind rage.

And hearing the girl's latch-key at a late hour,
reclines to troubled sleep in the weird moon
guilty, with fear appeased, and strangely turned
by light for a moment back to the girl who was won.

LOUIS JOHNSON

Fable of a Forgotten Woman

She has returned from Paris, I am told,
riddled with typhus, vastly pregnant, old
in the face and mind and clutching the arm
of a new, bewildered lover like a charm

that is wearing thin—fearful of her luck
and fearful in her eyes where the light leaks
onto her little secrets. Nothing has been
quite what she hoped for, and the obscene

images of her freedom no more amaze.
If she can count, her history is news
of several abortions and a round dozen men
and nothing worth doing, nor wish to have any again.

Nor does regret lurk in the hollow mind
remembering little, sensing a vast blur, blind
in the sun and afraid of the old friend, night—
where there is no more solace, and cold delight.

History is no more a story, but search for a cause—
something to blame—that rich house where a whore's
proclivities nurtured on finding everything easy
and struggle removed she was forced to replace with queasy

suffering, carnal experience—talking
meanwhile of life and art, of jazz, and stalking
a hidden self through jungles that were impassable
for the explorer stumbling back on her tracks from impossible

interiors, yet unable to rest. Failure she knew
would force her feet to itch and running away accrue
a fund of anecdote until, worn out, diseased,
all but that movement has gone, and her desperate death
    conceived.

LOUIS JOHNSON

Cataclysm

When, out of an intact sea rose terrible
a strange and menacing star that shook the ground
and lifted up the tides, man in that memorable
moment again fled to the mountain, to the gods forgotten:

And was again received though succour seemed
mythical through that long night of fire when the earth
burned, and higher waters rose: there was never dreamed
more nightmare sight than this organic act of birth,
whole villages dying, plantations sinking to shells
and herbage afloat to fructify petulant water: the wells
of the deep were broken up and the crazy sky
was a dawning red nightlong with the fires and the angry
planet flaming mad. It was, of course, the gods
had found man wanting by their measuring-rods.

But the one who came again from the mountain-top
in the wake of sinking water could not stop
praising the ordered heavens and the Gods' mercy
that had delivered him, till his songs' sorcery
forgot the sunken kingdoms and his drowned brothers
under his fervour and quick wife's breeding of others
who, simple enough, believed him too, and praised because
    they must
revere the force he said had made him first, from dust.

LOUIS JOHNSON

Poem in Karori
(*Thoughts of an elder*)

The proper fathers behind their ashen faces
survey with sparkless eyes the builded hills;
or, walking from the terminus, are stricken
by the reminding words a child has written
upon the path in chalk. Parchment conceals
(unfeeling sort of face) the memory-flashes.

'This way to the monkey's house'; he goes
like any wary child fearing the pointed finger
jibes out of nights and doorways; or
hearts etched where all will walk, stamp sure
on the soft feelings. He will not look at her
again in the morning now that the rough world knows.

Love is a taunt that no stern man may suffer.
Fear is a jibe that may be true. Admit
the guests now, from the dark mind forgotten.
Father, how old you look of a sudden
seeing a young man's fancy utters counterfeit
coins to pay for the one life you have to offer.

Suppose it were again true—you heard a child
call '*Kezia, wait for me!*' in these minor mountains;
these were not gateposts then, but boles of trees;
the humming trams—engines of climbing bees;
beneath the sailor-suit you are still uncertain
of what it will mean—or what it means to be foiled.

Say, we have flooded the margins with blithe prosperity;
the bankbooks all are volumes to be proud of:
children inhabit the dusk; are not the same as we were
when all the world was green as a song of pleasure.
'I must be old.' Impatience! Why this crowd of
useless ghosts attendant upon the day's equanimity?

Tonight I shall sit in the darkening room replete
and repeat—these children are not the same, but part
of that outer, rougher world I feared was growing up;
and reflect—in the face of it all, I drained a full cup.
The monkey's house is not the house of my heart;
another, another, will follow his fright up the street

LOUIS JOHNSON

Comedian

Faith of a kind is what a man prefers;
but he is left to find it by such means
rewards seem dubious: The desert airs,
the hungers and the panic are set scenes

along the way of ecstasy. Then some,
sensing a parallel, must raise a laugh
against the agonies of the machine:
and, by the paradox, achieve a half-

measure of truth while fumbling the clown's grail.
He is the smallest filament of light—
the god cut down. His fall, while others fail
to lift the load of rhetoric, is white

and flashed teeth in, he menace of the pit.
It's neither safe to say that he arrives,
nor pass him lightly off, who is the spit
fair in the eye of darkness while he lives.

He makes some pity for the human act
which may be useful. Harlequin in rags
totters—with all *our* tatters—through that tract
of tragedy that feeds love to the dogs.

Climbing the golden stairs, he'd surely trip
and rip the wings off angels as he fell.
Thus, though he may not reach the final step,
his grin must drag his breeches out of Hell.

LOUIS JOHNSON

The Sandwich Man

I am the man in the middle, the rare achievement
grown from a million pasts to a point of balance
between these wooden crusts of daily bread
feeding me and more than myself. I am the ornament
of the busy corner—jibe for the boy whose dance
is subsidised by graft that swarms in his home of the dead.

My function is first to amuse, and later instruct—
for my value is shock—with a price on my head—
there is always a moral in pity: my shoes are worn
wafers of charity—I am a willpower tacked
by despair to walk in the crowd and be read
as meek as you please, with a heavenly home to be won.

223

For I have inherited earth—beneath my thumbnail—
and know that the flesh must transcend the material.
I'm the senile edge of grandfather's progressive wish—
the torn smile of assurance that all will be well:
I am the clown in the grip of the ceremonial
terror—that without laughter darkness inherits the flesh.

Laugh if you will: all *will* be well—you can read!
The one who wrote my tunic is better-paid than you
and must surely know. Indeed, I know that there *is*,
even for rags and a bone, a love that is carried
as bright as sandwich-boards and twice as true:
and that a kiss can transform bitterness.

I could tell of a home of my own in another place
where a man could stand and praise: I still can stand,
and even my blame is an obverse praise—a plea
for another cheek to turn on the other side of my face—
for a hand that will again seek out my fortunate hand
and set the lightning-tongue of laughter free.

Laugh while you may; we yet may laugh together
and share the crusts of love in fairer weather.

RUTH DALLAS

Grandmother and Child

The waves that danced about the rock have gone,
The tide has stolen the rock as time has stolen
The quiet old lady who waited beneath the trees
That moved with a sad sea-sound in the summer wind.

When death was as near as the wind among the leaves,
Troubling the waking fear in the heart of the child
As the wind was troubling the shadows on the sunlit lawn,
The grandmother seemed as frail as the frailest leaf.

But she sat so still in the shade of the summer trees
With the wind of death on her cheeks and her folded hands,
Her strength seemed large and cool, as the rock in the sea
Seemed large and cool in the green and restless waves.

As the rock remains in the sea, deep down and strong,
The rock-like strength of the lady beneath the trees
Remains in the mind of the child, more real than death,
To challenge the child's strength in the hour of fear.

RUTH DALLAS

Milking before Dawn

In the drifting rain the cows in the yard are as black
And wet and shiny as rocks in an ebbing tide;
But they smell of the soil, as leaves lying under trees
Smell of the soil, damp and steaming, warm.
The shed is an island of light and warmth, the night
Was water-cold and starless out in the paddock.

Crouched on the stool, hearing only the beat
The monotonous beat and hiss of the smooth machines,
The choking gasp of the cups and rattle of hooves,
How easy to fall asleep again, to think
Of the man in the city asleep; he does not feel
The night encircle him, the grasp of mud.

225

But now the hills in the east return, are soft
And grey with mist, the night recedes, and the rain.
The earth as it turns towards the sun is young
Again, renewed, its history wiped away
Like the tears of a child. Can the earth be young again
And not the heart? Let the man in the city sleep.

RUTH DALLAS

Roads

Once it was difficult to keep to roads,
Ditches harboured nameless flowers, and sometimes
There were frogs and tadpoles in cold ponds.

Nowhere. The roads led nowhere then, and time
Was safely shut inside the clock at home.

Now to put time back inside the clock,
Now to be able to forget the signposts,
To rediscover pond and nameless flower.

Underneath the little bridges slow
Streams wandered, quiet willows grew.

But now the willows seem to hurry past us,
Drop between the folds of hills, and poplars
Seem to stride along like angry men.

Tussocks gallop by with flying manes,
And even hedges pass us, like long trains.

All that lingers, when the roads and hills
Have swung and swung away, is that one valley
Where at noon we boiled the billy, paused.

This alone remains, is here with stream
And tree and singing bird in this still room.

RUTH DALLAS

The World's Centre

The circle will remain, of mountain, hill
And curving sea that once enclosed the world,
And winds that smell and taste of the sea and shake
The needles from the pines with the sea's anger,
And great skies, and rivers blue as veins.

It is this landscape with the children walking
Small as starlings down beside the river,
And with the solitary small white launch
Like a folded gull, this bleak with water
Flax and tussock landscape that is passing.

This wilderness was pond and open flower,
The world's centre once, with nothing strange
In flax or tussock then, in trees all year
Carrying their leaves on stooping shoulders;
But moves further away as one grows older.

The pines along the yellow bank have turned
From cold sea winds towards the houses coming
Over the hills, the world that will not listen
To what the wind is saying and the water;
Soon the little trees, and flax, will follow.

All that once was here for ever seems
Hurrying away to be a tale
Told on a sunny doorstep, like the tales
Old men tell of vanished bush and mill,
That only children listen to and ponder.

RUTH DALLAS

Farmyard

He made a place in his dream for the pines to grow,
He saw their shadows lengthening, as now
In the slanting sun they lengthen, the house absorbing
Their still coolness; he saw the dogs asleep
Each in the shade of his kennel; weathered shafts
Resting on the ground, and big wheels resting.

These giant trees he saw spring from his hand,
And made a place in the air for them to grow,
A place for the low white house in their deep shelter;
But now if he could enter as once he entered
This cool yard, the dogs would suddenly rise,
Their barking shatter the dream and the sleepy stillness.

Nobody remembers him, the woman
Swinging her pail as she walks beneath great branches,
Going down through shade to the cool swept cowshed,
The man on the dusty roadside bringing the cows;
They do not know they follow the paths he made
In a dream once for a man and a woman to follow.

This is the resting centre, leaf and flower
Have budded from the dream, the roots have grown,
The earth has accepted the roots and the burden of wheels,
All is fulfilled; only the man who saw
In seedlings in his hand this quiet hour,
Has passed from the dream, passed from the trees' long
    shadows.

W. H. OLIVER

from Death and the Maiden

Mourn her in the valleys, you young lovers, and throughout
    your gloom
Sing her sad praises. For she is gone whom you could never
    love
Or cease from loving. She has taken a far stronger lover
To match her and mate her, your persons in all his ardours,
On a white bed, narrow and unpenitent, prepared for a new
    lord,
And one still older than ever comes to woman. She has laid
With her thin hands a skull between her breasts, and a knee
    of bone
Conquered her thighs where long you strove in hunger.
She has known love only in death, and he became lover
        To take her away.
Yet do not sing as if he conquered where you failed. He knew
No passion at the midnight, did not turn in the morning
And see with compassion her abandoned arms
Still hungry for him. Only when her sex had gone away
Was he triumphant, and the resistless morning knew his grief.
And now he's chained for ever at her feet
To watch her beauty move into the earth.

Sleep Will Come Singly

Sleep will come singly and the night will blind
With unnumbered fountains every troubled eye
And whisper solitude to crowded minds.

Sleep will be despot of these darkened hours
And wilfully administer his peace,
Till, recognized in dreams, the world is drowned

In a ghostly horde of petals and dead leaves.
Then will the meek man have his blood revived,
Tall as an antelope walk the bright fields,

Speak with a flower in his tongue, and listen to men
With a bird in the cage of his ear; on the limbs
Of impossible trees climb to heaven again.

Sleep will leave morning amazed with power,
And speaking from the high inchoate night
Will tell each little world its character.

W. H. OLIVER

The Phoenix

This red scabbard of rock
In hot December holds
Only a thread of water
Twisted along its folds.

The bitter summer leaves
No land unmarked, it locks
All life deep underground
Beneath the weight of rocks.

Echoes of torment travel
From hanging face to face
Across the parching gorges:
The seasons will displace

This death with chaos, though
In summer could arise
The flame-born phoenix, bright
And angered, soul's harsh prize.

W. H. OLIVER

The Beachcomber

Tall ships were wrecked here, and exotic cargoes
Spilled on the beach, not yet for the wave
And rock to disfigure, for the inquisitive gull to discard,
But for his delectation; for the space of an hour
Between tide and conquering tide
He could walk among an old world's refuse,
Decking worn smooth and bone fretted on rock,
Metal turned golden and red and shaped like small roses,
Run his fingers through them, until the whorled shell,
The ocean's own grace, became part of his own fancy;
And then walk homewards as the tide gathered,
With his head full of ghosts.
And the wild wave carried
Shells, bone and roses, into a common fortune
And walking homewards, he knew that the time was soon coming
When the wave would gather him also
And his white bones mingle
With that old imaginable world
Of roses hammered from gold and dyed with his own blood.

WILLIAM HART-SMITH

Holding-paddock

I followed a barbed-wire fence
to be cornered at last in a small
paddock sharpened to a point.

I walked out of it again, and round it
and left it behind, a crude arrangement of fence
tucked in a pine-dark corner of the world

otherwise fenceless and immense.
A very small holding-paddock,
its gate crooked on a loop hinge, open wide,

and nothing but dry dung,
cracked earth,
and thistles inside.

WILLIAM HART-SMITH

Shag Rookery

Now the cormorants are coming in to roost,
from beyond the town,
from up the coast and down,
all coming in to their rookery;

and I have upset things, upset the timetable,
caused hours of commotion in the sky
and over the darkening waters of the harbour
because I will not go away.

The first-comers, the early birds,
the young birds, and the oldsters looking for the best
    projection,
the grey young birds with the white feet,
and the dark old birds who fly heavily
and drop heavily
among the rafters of the beacon
and defend their places with hate—
some of these have settled in spite of me,
and they watch me
to see what I'm going to do.

The jagged rocks of the breakwater
are slashed and splashed with white excrement,
the dissolved bodies of countless fish
squirted from the bodies of fish-eating birds.
The rocks are white and greasy with an evil-smelling substance;
the stench and the isolation of these naked rocks
is their home, their leafless rookery
where they can sit above the sea
and croak themselves to sleep.

I shall not go yet,
I shall stand here until the sun finally goes
and the town is entirely submerged
in the fog that breathes up from the sea,
all except the spires
and the red lights of anchored vessels.
I shall stay here until the last fishing boat
that scuttles across the harbour mouth to home
is herself engulfed in the mist
and only the waves of her wash slap the rocks.

I shall stay here while the sky grows louder and louder
with the anxious whistle and throb of cormorant wings
and the troubled croak of the young.
When I decide to leave they will all come down
and dry their wings in the light of the beacon lamp.

WILLIAM HART-SMITH

Tractor

Dragging an iron rake
the tractor wallows
across the ocean of the paddock
with a fine excitement of gulls
in its wake.

It has two large paddle wheels,
a funnel, with smoke;
and the captain is on the bridge.
Having cast off a couple
of moments ago,
he sets a course for the opposite hedge.

WILLIAM HART-SMITH

The Shepherd and the Hawk

'Look here,' I said, 'Hawk,
you ugly old bird,
you scavenger.
What did you do to him?'
'Do what to whom?' said the hawk.

'I didn't do a thing!
Might as well blame
that white gull overhead.
I'm sorry for him.
See, he's printing himself
in black again
on the white sky.
It's because he's in mourning
for himself. Why?
Because he's just devoured his father.
Scavenger, you say!
What about him?
We don't believe in killing,
he and I.'

'What happened to that shepherd?'
I said. 'You know the one I mean,
the man who built himself a sod hut
and lived here
for years and years
but wouldn't let himself be seen.'

'Ha!' said the hawk
'that's a good one.
Fancy blaming me!
Your shepherd was original,
he ate his own
living heart for his tea!'

'That's a lie,' I said.
'The shepherd went mad,
that's all. It's a mortal habit.
From being alone so long
he took fright

235

from the packhorse man with the stores
and scuttled off like a rabbit
whenever he appeared.
And then one day
they found the stores untouched,
the shepherd dead.
What did you do with his heart, bird,
horrible bird?' I said.

'How near will I let you approach?'
said the evil-eyed bird
perched on the top wire.

'Try another step, I'll test myself;
you cannot hear my bird-heart beat
for the din of your own.'
Then he opened his wings,
orange-yellow on the underside.
I stopped, and he folded them again.

'I clean up your mess,'
said the hawk. 'And what have you done
with my little brothers and sisters
of the world's innocence?
Wasn't it you built this fence?'
said my hook-nosed tohunga.

'Hooks in the sky?' he said.
'Look, that's nothing.'
And opening his wings again, hauled
himself into the air, straight up,
hand over hand.

JAMES K. BAXTER

High Country Weather

Alone we are born
    And die alone;
Yet see the red-gold cirrus
    Over snow-mountain shine.

Upon the upland road
    Ride easy, stranger:
Surrender to the sky
    Your heart of anger.

JAMES K. BAXTER

The Antelopes

Beyond the edge of the world, past crater terrain
The lava flames and the volcanic rumble
Where the torn sky weeps iron for world's pain:
There in the ever-naked east remain
The gentle antelopes, a race undying
Who daylong wander on the autumn plain
Where the ripe grasses wake at noon and tremble
By winds fulfilled, regretting not their spring.

Over their dream domain the sun is steep;
And rock rings underfoot upon the hills.
Stirs there the fabled adder coiled asleep.
They pass unfearing torrent gorges deep

237

Meshing the thunder with their delicate cries.
One pool they drink from; then returning leap
Down to their grazing-ground. But now the cheetah kills
And lions darken evening with their eyes.

So when night falls these daylight children come
And huddle close beside the unknown tall
Stone amphitheatre at the desert's rim.
There moon rebuilds the wall with shadow beam.
But the frail creatures gazing cannot know
How vaster fear locks each loud crevice dumb.
Petrified anguish strains. The caverns still
With their dead gladiators horrent grow.

JAMES K. BAXTER

Tunnel Beach

The waist high sea was rolling
Thunder along her seven iron beaches
When we climbed down to rocks and the curved sand,
Drowned Lyonesse lay lost and tolling
Waiting the cry of the sun's phoenix
From the sea carved cliffs that held us in their hand.

Forgotten there the green
Paddocks we walked an hour before,
The mare and the foal and the witch tormented wood
And the flaked salt boughs, for the boughs of flame were seen
Of the first garden and the root
Of graves in your salt mouth and the forehead branded fire.

Through the rock tunnel whined
The wind, Time's hound in leash,
And stirred the sand and murmured in your hair,
The honey of your moving thighs
Drew down the cirrus sky, your doves about the beach
Shut out sea thunder with their wings and stilled the lonely
    air.

But O rising I heard the loud
Voice of the sea's women riding
All storm to come. No virgin mother bore
My heart wave eaten. From the womb of cloud
Falls now no dove, but combers grinding
Break sullen on the last inviolate shore.

JAMES K. BAXTER

To My Father

Today, looking at the flowering peach,
The island off the shore and waves that break
Quiet upon the rocks and level beach—
We must join forces, you and I, remake
The harbour silted and the city bombed
And all our hopes that lie now fire-entombed.

Your country childhood helped to make you strong,
Ploughing at twelve. I only know the man.
While I grew up more sheltered and too long
In love with my disease; though illness can
Impart by dint of pain a different kind
Of toughness to the predatory mind.

There is a feud between us. I have loved
You more than my own good, because you stand
For country pride and gentleness, engraved
In forehead lines, veins swollen on the hand;
Also behind slow speech and quiet eye
The rock of passionate integrity.

You were a poet whom the time betrayed
To action. So, as Jewish Solomon
Prayed for wisdom, you had prayed
That you might have a poet for a son.
The prayer was answered; but an answer may
Confound by its exactness those who pray.

Finding no fault in you, I have been tempted
To stay your child. But that which broke
(Nature) the navel-cord, has not exempted
Even your light and sympathetic yoke.
It is in me your own true mettle shows;
Nor can we thus be friends till we are foes.

This you know well, but it will bear repeating—
Almost you are at times a second self;
Almost at times I feel your heart beating
In my own breast as if there were no gulf
To sever us. And you have seemed then rather
An out-of-time twin brother than a father.

So much is true; yet I have seen the time
When I would cut the past out like a cancer
Which now I must digest in awkward rhyme
Until I move 'in measure like a dancer'.
To know an age where all our loves have scope:
It is too much for any man to hope.

You, tickling trout once in a water-race;
You, playing cards, not caring if you lost;
You, shooting hares high on the mountain face;
You, showing me the ferns that grow from frost;
You, quoting Burns and Byron while I listened;
You, breaking quartz until the mica glistened.

These I remember, with the wind that blows
For ever pure down from the tussock ranges;
And these remain, like the everlasting snows,
Changeless in me while my life changes;
These and a thousand things that prove
You rooted like a tree in the land's love.

I shall compare you to the bended bow,
Myself the arrow launched upon the hollow
Resounding air. And I must go
In time, my friend, to where you cannot follow.
It is not love would hope to keep me young,
The arrow rusted and the bow unstrung.

We have one aim: to set men free
From fear and custom and the incessant war
Of self with self and city against city—
So they may know the peace that they were born for
And find the earth sufficient, who instead
For fruit give scorpions and stones for bread.

And I sit now beside the wishing-well
And drop my silver down. I will have sons
And you grandchildren yet to tell
Old tales despite the anger of the guns:
Leisure to stroll and see Him unafraid
Who walked with Adam once in the green shade.

JAMES K. BAXTER

Elegy for an Unknown Soldier

There was a time when I would magnify
His ending; scatter words as if I wept
Tears not my own but man's; there was a time.
But not now so. He died of a common sickness.

Nor did any new star shine
Upon that day when he came crying out
Of fleshy darkness to a world of pain,
And waxen eyelids let the daylight enter.

So felt and tasted, found earth good enough.
Later he played with stones and wondered
If there was land beyond the dark sea rim
And where the road led out of the farthest paddock.

Awkward at school, he could not master sums.
Could you expect him then to understand
The miracle and menace of his body
That grew as mushrooms grow from dusk to dawn?

He had the weight, though, for a football scrum,
And thought it fine to listen to the cheering
And drink beer with the boys, telling them tall
Stories of girls that he had never known.

So when the War came he was glad and sorry,
But soon enlisted. Then his mother cried
A little, and his father boasted how
He'd let him go, though needed for the farm.

Likely in Egypt he would find out something
About himself, if flies and drunkenness
And deadly heat could tell him much—until
In his first battle a shell splinter caught him.

So crown him with memorial bronze among
The older dead, child of a mountainous island.
Wings of a tarnished victory shadow him
Who born of silence has burned back to silence.

JAMES K. BAXTER

Wild Bees

Often in summer on a tarred bridge plank standing
Or downstream between willows, a safe Ophelia drifting
In a rented boat—I had seen them come and go,
Those wild bees swift as tigers, their gauze wings a-glitter
In passionless industry, clustering black at the crevice
Of a rotten cabbage tree, where their hive was hidden low.

But never strolled too near. Till one half-cloudy evening
Of ripe January, my friends and I
Came, gloved and masked to the eyes like plundering
    desperadoes
To smoke them out. Quiet beside the stagnant river
We trod wet grasses down, hearing the crickets chitter
And waiting for light to drain from the wounded sky.

Before we reached the hive their sentries saw us
And sprang invisible through the darkening air;
Stabbed, and died in stinging. The hive woke. Poisonous
    fuming

Of sulphur filled the hollow trunk, and crawling
Blue flame sputtered: yet still their suicidal
Live raiders dived and clung to our hands and hair.

O it was Carthage under the Roman torches
Or loud with flames and falling timber, Troy.
A job well botched: half of the honey melted
And half the rest young grubs. Through earth-black
   smouldering ashes
And maimed bees groaning, we drew out our plunder—
Little enough their gold, and slight our joy.

Fallen then the city of instinctive wisdom.
Tragedy is written distinct and small:
A hive burned on a cool night in summer.
But loss is a precious stone to me, a nectar
Distilled in time, preaching the truth of winter
To the fallen heart that does not cease to fall.

JAMES K. BAXTER

The Hermit

Where the salt creek broadens to a brown lagoon
Fringed with matted swordgrass and seawrack,
There in a corrugated iron shack
Behind a brushwood fence, he lives alone—
The odd-job man, old bludger, worn-out soak,
Hoeing spuds in his garden on the dune
Or mowing lawns by the summer cribs of townsfolk.

Three children married and a wife dead,
He has little enough to live for, one would say.
In mine and thrashing-mill he had his day

Bullocking, a strong back and weak head
(Pipe music, Irish whisky, quids to spend)
Now lies rheumatic in his stretcher bed
Feeling the raw cold and his nearing end.

The rotten boards are barely weatherproof,
Grey spiders scuttle in the draught and damp.
Late in the evening by his spirit lamp,
'I am the Resurrection and the Life'
He reads, thumbing a worn Bible page—
And when the kids throw pebbles on his roof
Smiles, and remembers his own sapling age.

Then, as his eyes fail in the growing dusk,
Kneels down upon a sacking rug and prays,
His heart like wax in God's meridian blaze,
His body shaken like a burnt-out husk:
Praises that Love who wakened him to weep
When drawn vertiginous in a deathly masque
By *ignis fatuus* and the smell of sleep.

Morning finds him on his daily round,
Stripping black mussels from a tide-swept ledge
Or clipping fronds from the macrocarpa hedge
That guards some well-fed bookie's house and ground.
And soon a wave will take him, or the cold
March gales, his lean flesh in a sodden mound,
His spent soul to that river where none grow old.

JAMES K. BAXTER

Poem in the Matukituki Valley

Some few yards from the hut the standing beeches
Let fall their dead limbs, overgrown
With feathered moss and filigree of bracken.
The rotted wood splits clean and hard
Close-grained to the driven axe; with sound of water
Sibilant falling and high nested birds.

In winter blind with snow; but in full summer
The forest blanket sheds its cloudy pollen
And cloaks a range in undevouring fire.
Remote the land's heart; though the wild scrub cattle
Acclimatized, may learn
Shreds of her purpose, or the taloned kea.

For those who come as I do, half-aware,
Wading the swollen
Matukituki waist-high in snow water,
And stumbling where the mountains throw their dice
Of boulders huge as houses, or the smoking
Cataract flings its arrows on our path—

For us the land is matrix and destroyer
Resentful, darkly known
By sunset omens, low words heard in branches;
Or where the red deer lift their innocent heads
Snuffing the wind for danger,
And from our footfall's menace bound in terror.

Three emblems of the heart I carry folded
For charms against flood water, sliding shale—
Pale gentian, lily, and bush orchid.

The peaks too have names to suit their whiteness,
Stargazer and Moonraker,
A sailor's language or a mountaineer's.

And those who sleep in close bags fitfully
Besieged by wind in a snowline bivouac:
The carrion parrot with red underwing
Clangs on the roof by night; and daybreak brings
Raincloud on purple ranges, light reflected
Stainless from crumbling glacier, dazzling snow.

Do they not, clay in that unearthly furnace,
Endure the hermit's peace
And mindless ecstasy? Blue-lipped crevasse
And smooth rock chimney straddling—a communion
With what eludes our net: Leviathan
Stirring to ocean birth our inland waters?

Sky's purity, the altar cloth of snow
On deathly summits laid; or avalanche
That shakes the rough moraine with giant laughter;
Snowplume and whirlwind—what are these
But His flawed mirror, who gave the mountain strength
And dwells in holy calm, undying freshness?

Therefore we turn, hiding our souls' dullness
From that too blinding glass: turn to the gentle
Dark of our human daydream, child and wife,
Patience of stone and soil, the lawful city
Where man may live, and no wild trespass
Of what's eternal shake his grave of time.

JAMES K. BAXTER

Rocket Show

As warm north rain breaks over suburb houses
Streaming on window glass, its drifting hazes
Covering harbour ranges with a dense hood—
I recall how eighteen months ago I stood
Ankle-deep in sand on an Otago beach
Watching the fireworks flare over strident surf and bach,
In brain grey ash, in heart the seachange flowing
Of one love dying and another growing.

  For love grows like the crocus bulb in winter
Hiding from snow and from itself the tender
Green frond in embryo; but dies as rockets die
(White sparks of pain against a steel dark sky)
With firebird wings trailing an arc of grief
Across a night inhuman as the grave,
Falling at length a dull and smouldering shell
To frozen dunes or the wash of the quenching swell.

    There was little room left where the crowd had trampled
Grass and lupin bare, under the pines that trembled
In gusts from the sea. On a sandhillock I chose
A place to watch from . . . Then the rockets rose
O marvellous, like self-destroying flowers
On slender stems, with seed-pods full of flares
Raining down amber, scarlet, pennies from heaven
On the skyward straining heads and still sea-haven.
Had they brought death, we would have stood the same
I think, in ecstasy at the world-end flame.

    It is the rain streaming reminds me of
Those ardent showers, cathartic love and grief.

As I walked home through the cold streets by moonlight,
My steps ringing in the October night,
I thought of our strange lives, the grinding cycle
Of death and renewal come to full circle;
And of man's heart, that blind Rosetta stone,
Mad as the polar moon, decipherable by none.

JAMES K. BAXTER

Tarras Moon

When Tim and I stumbled
On the rough Tarras track
(We shared the station shack)
Blind drunk we fumbled
Like ferrets in a sack
Together tumbled,
That no way can fare.

I knew her not from a lantern
Or a lowe in the lift—
Grim in her graveshift
The bare poxy wanton,
Queen Death glowered from a rift
Of cloudwrack above the mountain,
Walking on wild air.

'Ripe archaic' her feature
From a Sicilian metope,
Two snakes for a knotted rope
About her middle: the creature
That eats our carrion hope:
Glass of malignant Nature,
Diana chastely fair.

'She's like my granny, but older
By a long chalk,' Tim said.
In a corpselight hither shed
Clear shone tussock and boulder:
Like men already dead
Under Mt. Iron's shoulder
Moonstruck we staggered there.

JAMES K. BAXTER

from Cressida

1.   *In the Lecture Room*

The lecturer's impartial prose
  Droned in the raftered room;
Through a mock-Gothic window rose
  The soft weir water's boom.

The blonde girl in the second bench
  Biting her pencil, sighed—
Thought 'If I lowered my frock an inch
  It would look well in that shade'.

The young man at the back, half-turning
  To see her profile, smiled;
Thought 'She has a scholar's learning
  And the innocence of a child'.

The clock in the college tower broke
  On sparrows' private lives:
The lecturer cleared his throat and spoke
  Of McDougall's instinctive drives;

Paused a moment in his talk,
  Massaged an itching wen,
Doodled a diagram in chalk
  And rubbed it off again.

v. *Her First Song*

What's silver and a house to me
If I with my own love agree?
Any old coat would do to cover
Us from the night, alive, aglow;
But all are cold who lack a lover.
Time is like the falling snow.

Though he tell me yet again
And a hundred times in vain
For his going is good reason,
How can barren Reason know
Love's mysterious tide and season.
Time is like the falling snow.

He may meet another there,
Forget that I am fond and fair:
Absent faces lose their colour
Lacking scope for love to grow,
Mind estranged and memory duller.
Time is like the falling snow.

One song have I at daybreak heard
From the throat of the waking bird.
Tell it in my true love's chamber,
Tell him truth: *None can blow*
Fire from the fading ember:
Time is like the falling snow.

251

VI. *The Parting*

The drizzling murk of a March dawn:
Girder, bridge and signal tower
Bald on a raw sky yellow-dun.
The clock hands inching toward the hour
Pause, Time's systole in reverse;
The engine is a plumed hearse.

Upon the station wall a torn
Poster like a banner flaps:
Impossible valleys gold with corn,
Cloud-cuckoo-land, where no mishaps
Of grief or unfaith change the scene
Of trysting to a black ravine.

But the clock tells of here and now.
A usual couple walk
The platform, scarved—tearmarks show
Upon her cheeks, though calm they talk.
This, in the glass of a grievous dream.
—Their voices drown in the hiss of steam.

IX. *Her Second Song*

The books grow clear upon the shelf,
Locke, Berkeley, Hume.
The wind loves no one but itself
That sings outside a rented room
And rustles in the lilac tree—
O my dear and only.

I had a love who pleased me well
(*Locke, Berkeley, Hume*)
He left me single for a spell.

Brief and brisk it seemed to him
But a long dry road it was to me—
  Yes, my dear and only.

Once work and fancy were enough
  (*Locke, Berkeley, Hume*)
Few to speak to, none to love,
Easy go, easy come—
Till you and I touched knee to knee,
  Yes, my dear and only.

Three white angels at my head,
  Locke, Berkeley, Hume.
One stands at the foot of the bed:
Black Abaddon is his name,
He is stronger than the other three,
  O my dear and only.

XI. *Her Decision*

Show me the face, cold mirror, that the world
Can see and prize: myself you'll never show.
Eyes wide apart, forehead a trifle low,
Rose-ruddy cheeks, the ripe mouth cupid-curled.
Blonde hair, they say, *is fickle*: I'm a blonde.
Then I'll stay home and read a book tonight;
Let him tire waiting, walk the lawn in spite.
They say, *Fidelity's a standing pond*
(But I'll not listen). How the mean thoughts swarm
Like flies in sunlight, sparks behind a grate!
It was not so: too much alone of late
I grow unsure. The waste wind blowing warm

Can ruffle the deep well of happiness
But never dry it. Oh the moon controls
Our sex, the subtle mercury our souls!
—The amber necklace then, and the grey dress.

XII. *Lounge Bar*

A night that smells of sailor's tar.
The lightshade swings above the bar;
The wound throbs beneath the scar.

Wind blow hot, wind blow cold:
All that glitters is not gold,
The body young, the mind old.

Ill comes of what in play began—
Grief and the horoscope of man
Contracted to a glass's span.

A grinning quicksand hides beneath
When he and I mix breath with breath,
Though gin can mask the taste of death.

Here where the puppet-wires strum
Thought narrows and the heart is numb;
But when to a private place we come,

Then flesh on flesh will strike a spark—
From pole to icy pole an arc,
A bridge on the unfaithful dark.

I may suppose till dawn's grimace
That his face is another's face,
Myself a bride in wedding lace.

254

xv. *Sestina*

Swept clean of leaves, with stripped boughs, the garden
Lifts black arms to the wan sky of winter,
Mater Dolorosa: the orchid house
Shuttered, and no birds by the pond's clear glass
Where the boy and dolphin stand, to summer constant
Rapt yet in the daze of an archaic dream.

Here was my hope planted, the virgin dream
Of evergreen amazement, a snakeless garden.
By my own fault, to true love unconstant
I chart now an iron graph of winter;
Or, Hans Andersen's mermaid, walk on glass,
On thorns, hot ploughshares, through a charnel house.

But you, stranger, in my body's house
Sheltered, dreaming your deepwater dream,
Who make my shape strange in a looking-glass:
You, curled in the dusk of the first garden,
Forgive me if I call your weight a winter,
Castaway, to an older sun constant.

The flesh may be infirm, the spirit constant,
Though none know this in parlour or priest's house.
You, conceived in an icy absence, winter
Of sight, sound, touch, are substance of that dream
I dreamt when first I walked an autumn garden
And foresaw lasting joy in a lying glass.

Were he love's kind, to see without a glass,
He would be constant yet to me inconstant,
Forgive as one did in Gethsemane's garden;

But here are shapes lewd in a haunted house—
I am alone, locked in the glacial dream
Of those who wake and know the world's winter.

Lie still, child of unfaith—soon comes Winter,
Though you fear nothing, in the womb's dark glass
Withheld: storm, tremor, cannot shake your dream;
Nor shall drug shatter. To your own law constant,
Fly whorled in amber, sleep—to a warring house
You will wake soon, and an unfruitful garden.

—I had not thought, garden, that I would winter
In the ill planet's house. Prediction's glass
Is flawed by our inconstant waking dream.

JAMES K. BAXTER

The Homecoming

Odysseus has come home, to the gully farm
Where the macrocarpa windbreak shields a house
Heavy with time's reliques—the brownfilmed photographs
Of ghosts more real than he; the mankind-measuring arm
Of a pendulum clock; and true yet to her vows,
His mother, grief's Penelope. At the blind the sea wind
    laughs.

The siege more long and terrible than Troy's
Begins again. A Love demanding all,
Hypochondriacal, seadark and contentless:
This was the sour ground that nurtured a boy's
Dream of freedom: this, in Circe's hall
Drugged him; his homecoming finds this, more relentless.

She does not say 'You have changed'; nor could she imagine any
Otherwise to the quiet maelstrom spinning
In the circle of their days. Still she would wish to carry
Him folded within her, shut from the wild and many
Voices of life's combat, in the cage of beginning;
She counts it natural that he should never marry.

She will cook his meals; complain of the south weather
That wrings her joints. And he—rebels; and yields
To the old covenant—calms the bleating
Ewe in birth travail. The smell of saddle leather
His sacrament; or the sale day drink; yet hears beyond sparse
    fields
On reef and cave the sea's hexameter beating.

JAMES K. BAXTER

Never No More

Oh the summer's afloat on spindrift beaches
Brown as bread in a holiday heaven:
The same sweet lie the lupin teaches
As always dropping her gay pollen
On a girl's print frock leg shoulder bare
Never no more, never no more.

The boys climb to their branch high houses
Under a black bridge dive for pennies
The noon cloud like a bird's breast downy
Night come cool as a hawthorn berry
Kite tails tied on a telephone wire
Never no more, never no more.

Cigarette stink from a hole in the rushes
Dark as a dunny the under-runner
The green flax plaited for whiplashes
Cockabully finned with the fire of summer
Jack loves Jill on the garage door
Never no more, never no more.

The trodden path in the brambles led
Sweet and sure to a lifted frock
To the boathouse spree and the hayloft bed
A hamstrung heart and no way back:
Like a toi-toi arrow shot in the air
Never no more, never no more.

JAMES K. BAXTER

Mill Girl

Attendant angel, mark this one
Fresh as paint in the flower of her sixteenth year:
With sheltering wing surround her. The great loom she
Tends, like a monstrous child—its bellowings stun,
Drug, drown her mind like the drumming of a weir;
Her heart's yet innocent of time's captivity.

Nor does she see behind the eyes that feed
On her rose, rash nubility (the tough boys
Who yarn, mending the broken bobbin-strings)
A tigerish jungle of incontinent need,
A cobra's nonchalance swaying at poise,
A bar room vanity that blinks and springs.

258

She waits in the ignorant garden of her wishes
Till Mr Right (first glimpsed in *The Oracle*) come
Darkhaired and smiling to take her ungloved hand
And lead her into a world lovely as fishes,
Secret as starlight, out of the stagnant slum
She knows, the flyspecked kitchen, to a table at the Grand.

Though Love cannot save, at least it will watch and weep
On that near night when she, under a moonless sky
On wet park leaves, or on a mattress in a back
Room at the party, loses what none can keep—
Rough and ready, before the keg runs dry
Fumbled and forced—yet willing, ready to learn the knack.

JAMES K. BAXTER

Seraphion

I, Seraphion, hermit of Mount Athos,
Three hundred feet above the sea's mumble
Alone in a rock shelter, the sparrow's refuge,
With a stone couch, one ikon and a lamp,
In the judgment of the eye of absolute Day
Await the hour of my death.

I, Seraphion, was once Demetrios
Singer of ballads, thief and actor.
Lord, let these swollen joints, back bruised by the scourge,
Eyes weak with tears and icy fasting,
Be acceptable sacrifice, sign of the penitent—Deliver,
O Lord, my soul alive!

Tzv

This voice, whose psalms startle the gull, once
In wineshops won silver and applause; these knees, that bend
Hourly, in the pit of perfumed beds
Opened the thighs of harlots. In Alexandrian gardens,
In the brothels of Beirut, in the mire of Babylon
My invisible Enemy triumphed, and trod me down.

Till in black night came One, the Shepherd, to wash me
Clean of the burning raddle. Let Him be praised:
With Him alone is power. I woke and fled
To the rock of Athos, shunning
All temporal beauty, solace of wall and vineyard
To praise Him in the desert of His Truth.

On Athos is no sight or sound of woman,
No female thing, no, not a pigeon cloistered
On monastery roofs. In this bare place
My hermitage, I see only at evening
The face of him who brings me water and lentils,
Kneels for my blessing, and goes, with no word said.

But at night a voice comes on the wind, a phantom
Torments me, touching my ageing limbs with fire:
A sea boy out of Smyrna. Two years we lived
In unlawful love, thieving and drinking together,
Till he left me for a wealthy Lebanese
For a new overcoat, and a villa in Cairo.

With mouth of pomegranate, with skin of jessamine,
With eyes like wintry flowers, with cheeks firm as olives,
With corrupt blood, with the treachery of a panther.
Two years we lived at loggerheads together.
In his flesh I embraced the flesh of the young Hyakinthos,
And between midnight and morning he taunts me still.

ALISTAIR CAMPBELL

Narcissus

At the great water's edge
    Golden Narcissus lies;
Hand propped under his chin,
    Bees at his thighs;
His eyes fixed upon nothing
    Where his image lies.
        O Echo, Echo.

Like the neck of a swan,
    In the indifferent stream
The other hand trails;
    Sleek as cream
Are his dimpled cheeks;
    His plump mouth dreams.
        O Echo, Echo.

The bruised flower of his mouth
    The honey-bee stings;
Rain in his small delicious ears
    Like a dragonfly sings
At noon; between his toes
    The grasshopper springs.
        O Echo, Echo.

Closes a blue-veined lid
    Upon velvet eyes;
Falls the sleek head; falls
    The hand from the thighs;
From the brimming mirror dim
    The image flies.
        O Echo, Echo.

In his great golden helmet
    The small wren builds;
To the bee his rotten rich mouth
    Sweet honey yields:
This proud young man like a stag
    Once trod these fields.
        O Echo, Echo.

For this is great Narcissus
    Who moulders here;
Watercress grows from his eyes
    And grass from his ears;
From his thigh a honey-sleek flower
    At its image stares.
        O Echo, Echo.

ALISTAIR CAMPBELL

At the Fishing Settlement

October, and a rain-blurred face
Walking, walking into the sea. The place
Was a bare sea-battered town
With its single street leading down
Onto a gravel beach. Sea-winds
Had long picked the hills clean
Of everything but tussock and stones,
And pines that dropped small brittle cones
Onto a soured soil. And old houses flanking
The street hung poised like driftwood planking
Blown together and could not outlast
The next window-shuddering blast

From the storm-whitened sea.
It was bitterly cold; I could see
Where muffled against gusty spray
She walked the clinking shingle; a stray
Dog whimpered, and pushed its small
Wet nose into my hand;—that is all.
Yet I am haunted by that face,
That dog, and that bare bitter place.

ALISTAIR CAMPBELL

Now He is Dead

Now he is dead, who talked
Of wild places and skies
Inhabited by the hawk;

Of the hunted hare that flies
Down bare parapets of stone,
And there closes its eyes;

Of trees fast-rooted in stone
Winds bend but cannot break;
Of the low terrible moan

That dead thorn-trees make
On a windy desolate knoll;
Of the storm-blackened lake,

Where heavy breakers roll
Out of the snow-bred mist,
When the glittering air is cold;

Of the Lion Rock that lifts
Out of the whale-backed waves
Its black sky-battering cliffs;

Of the waterfall that raves
Down the dark mountain side,
And into a white cauldron dives.

ALISTAIR CAMPBELL

Now Sleeps the Gorge

Now sleeps the gorge, the pale moon's steaming disk
Desolate and glimmering through the gusty mist;
The storm that through the wind-cropt tussock
Screams, and screams where the great hawks rest

Upon comfortless stone their arrogant hearts;
Now sleeps the mist whose tumbling woods unroll
Upon gullied hills, and with the dawn depart;
The streaming woods, the pigeon-moaning knoll,

And swarming under cliffs like smoking swords,
The rock-torn Clutha. O this bare place
Embalms such glory, beast nor bird of day
Walks or flies but in its living grace.

ALISTAIR CAMPBELL

Lie on the Sand

Lie on the sand, my dazzling driftwood;
Root toes and fingers into burning sand and cling
While the sun makes a satin coat of your skin,
And brings the beaded sweat on lip and chin.

Is not the mind but a beehive then,
And thought, the honey that drips from the cell
When the bee has not will to stir a wing
But pants where it huddles from scathing skies? . . .

Time crystallizes with the molten sun
Within this crucible of rock and pool,
Into an artifice of the dreaming mind
Where perfect thoughts like bees in amber lie.

ALISTAIR CAMPBELL

O Catch Miss Daisy Pinks

O catch Miss Daisy Pinks
Undressing behind her hair;
She slides open like a drawer
Oiled miraculously by a stare.

O the long cool limbs,
The ecstatic shot of hair,
And untroubled eyes
With their thousand mile stare.

265

Her eyes are round as marigolds;
Her navel drips with honey;
Her pulse is even, and her laugh
Crackles like paper money.

ALISTAIR CAMPBELL

Hut Near Desolated Pines

Cobwebs and dust have long
Deadened an old man's agony.
The choked fireplace, the chair
On its side on the mud floor,
May have warmed an old man's
Bones or propped them upright
While his great head nodded;
Fantastical images may have stirred
His mind when the wind moaned
And sparks leapt up the chimney
With a roar. But what great gust
Of the imagination threw wide
The door and smashed the lamp
And overturned both table and chair? . . .
A rabbiter found him sprawled
By the door; no violence, nothing
To explain, but the hungry rats
That scurried over the fouled straw.
A foolish lonely old man
With dung matted into his beard.
Since when birds stuffed the chimney
With straw, and a breeze flapped
Continually through the sack window;

And all the while the deft spiders
Doodled away at their obituaries,
And the thin dust fell from the rafters . . .
Nothing but cobwebs and dust
Sheeting an old man's agony.

KEITH SINCLAIR

The Chronicle of Meola Creek

Not I, some child, born in a marvellous year,
Will learn the trick of standing upright here.
Allen Curnow
Yet many do live their lives here as natives.
T. H. Scott, *Landfall 6*

I

We both were five and we both were wild
With the summer-time hung on the mudflats that lay,
Each holiday morning, for the world of our play,
When I showed Ngaire the way to sea,
That black-haired bride of a child.

Our schooners sailed, a loving pair,
Down the channel that steered through the Sargasso Sea,
Past the corals, the cannibal isles, and the tree
With roots that fed in the sea-bed scrub
And leaves that sucked from the air.

The sea-grass snatched at our laden keels
As they scored their deep trails in the skin of the bay,
As we opened our hatches to spill our array
Of tribute paid by the lands we had sailed
To the Rock our wonder revealed.

We sang happy end to the ocean's track,
Sang hail to the Rock of the farthermost fame,
To the desperate Rock with the dangerous name
That called its sailors back.

We rejoiced at the end of the day-long play
That the worlds we created were dead as we left,
And the silence, unpeopled, awaited our breath
On the beach that we owned every day.

II

Alan and I were the marlin's fins
In the milk of our youth as we furrowed and flew,
While the salt came like curd in the wake our canoe
Had arrowed wide on the narrow tide,
And the sun was thick on our skins.

We hailed the bush on the hallowed hill
Where the Maoris surrounded the Volunteers' fort,
And the Rangers had died for the England they sought
In the fern they claimed for their sons to burn,
The silt they hungered to till.

We jumped the wall of each wave that bucked
Round the petulant turns of the lava-fed creek,
And we crossed the Pacific in less than a week.
We slipped the teeth of the eel-like reef
To the Point where the garfish hooked.

We were glad in the myth that was breast to our mouth,
That was home, where our play was, with coastline and
   paddock,
We were *Tainui* and *Tory* that nosed out the hot,
Sad latitudes of south.

268

Where they hoped for homes in the jaws of the pole
We raised our dreams on a point of loam,—
The statues of men who grew famous at home
When the south was a future and soul.

III

When we were the people our time had grown,
The poet, the artist, the prophet we meant,
We launched our youth in the flames of the men
And the mangroves, meeting along the creek,
The towns that our eyes had known.

We were brave, were mapping the coasts of mind
Where we strove to plant, in the soil of speech,
The truth that was born on a Rock, a Creek:
Our random home, grown native now,
Was the pith in life that our past assigned.

Our minds were making the shape of years.
Though our fathers had never been older than boys,
In a land where the flesh, without spirit, enjoyed
Eternal riches without growing rich,
We sailed future, older years.

As the dung in the earth and the rotting bark
Are the womb of the rose, so the grossness of flesh
That had swelled in the south, was the threshold
Of thinking eyes in the mindless dark.

The Islands were named in that bright metastasis.
The renewed zeal and sun of September
Had marked them the next of the last, and a member
Of the cities of Athens and Cnossos.

They were harbour, were shelter, were shell,
While an orchid constricted its petals of frost
Round the red, red mainlands the migrants lost
When they followed the summer for dwelling.

Where they shifted their roofs and their speech
To the sun in the south, their dreams followed,
And—banned by the tides from the sorrows
Of continents—rooted in bracken and beach.

Poems grew outward like love from the yolk
That embraced the whole of their living lives.
Their abstractions were native and wived
By the beauty their land bespoke.

The Islands were the bows of all ships,
But they called no sailors home, for no sons left
The cross of the south, that was weft
To the warp of the world's apocalypse.

KEITH SINCLAIR

Moors, Angels, Civil Wars

Not the angelic host of Moors were the foe,
Nor the general, his dying body a balloon,
But the past, the migrations, civil wars,
The invaders, Romans, Visigoths,
The weight of the Church evangelist
And militant against all sins,
Even as small as the unseen son
Conceived some hot forgotten night,
The bars closed and the moon risen.

270

The victories were temporary, unwilling,
Since we shipped our cause, to fight for it
In a foreign land, since we could not win
In a life of time, nor lose lost hope.
Seeking martyrdom, not triumphs,
Believing in the blood, the pulse, the eye,
Seeing a cathedral of fair flesh,
We few, we daring few, revolted,
Grew closer in fear and whispers than in love.

What though the cause were lost before
The war? All was not lost, the sneer,
The defiant word, the blackamoor's swagger—
Brother before the missionary foe.
A horde of conspirators yet unborn
Would bleed for the freedom of the blood to burn.
Plots, rebellions, poisoners would breed,
Young eyes shine to hear how we died,
And we, the first, would lead a fleet
Of love to the longed embrace, life's kisses;
To the expected landing, all beauty in our ships;
To battle, all evil in their falling towns,
All lying, death, all the no, the no;
In our hands such a bright, O dreaming love, a sword.

．　　　　．　　　　．

They hound me down the Ramblas, past
The foot in the door, the eye behind
The blind, across the toadstool square
In Santa Eulalia's shadows. Through the grid
In the cellar I watch black boots
Pass by, the young deprived of life,
The poor affirming poverty.
Then, with a rattle of arms, caught.

I fire in their faces and not death, not bullets,
Water spits from the pistol mouth.
Back to the black Inquisitors, and the no,
No answers, only a memory of past
Hills dim through the glass of pain.

Suddenly there in the white room
And brighter than the electric light, wings
Sprout round my ears. O laughing
I fly through the castle window, past
The town, along the Costa Brava,
Parakeet riding the waves of air
To the last of my secret friends alive.
Fiend, he holds death out like a gift,
The drink he gives is acid in my eyes.
Fly faster back to the honest torture
Of the black guards, and the white-gowned
Doctors' medicines; sweet swallow down.

KEITH SINCLAIR

A Night Full of Nothing

We met in a bushel of paradise birds
While the cockatoo langled his whimsical lay.
I garbled her mouth for a wonder of words,
O why did she linger and why did she stay?

Her breasts were a gallon of gathering bees
And lily legs walked her down lover's delay
As we ripened like raspberries high in the trees,
O why did she linger and why did she stay?

She was the mare all a-meadowed with spring
And I was a night-time of lances to slay
In the lists of her limbs, in her laughter my ring,
O why did she linger and why did she stay?

We larked it, we liked it, all play-timing on,
It was dripping with moonshine from kiss to doomsday
One night full of nothing and then she was gone,
O why did she linger and why did she stay?

KEITH SINCLAIR

Mother

She sits with a son on her nursery knee
With never a breast to call her own,
More ancient than evil and further from me
Than ever were angels or idols.

A moon to her sun and his star

She walks in a cloud of nesting wings
And no hawk, not I, can pirate there,
In the world the narcotic of infancy brings
Where loneliness has no name.

A moon to her sun and his star

Where did he come from this amorous boy
Who is houses of lovers and satisfied never?
He came from my company lodging with joy
And left me to talk to myself.

A moon to her sun and his star

273

For a Parting

They are gone who were the sum of summer
And the calendar of wishes cannot number
The days that the winter of waiting will hold.
Mind and blood are numbed, I am old,
For absence is an evening more ageing than years.
They are gone the centre of my hemisphere
Which flies apart like a flight of birds
Diluted by the shot-gun's burst.

He who befriends a man has half of life
But he who is loved by a man and his wife
Has the skylark's score and the upper air,
Has a Saturday singing the song for his words.
They are gone who made life's mixture hold
Together, with more memories than I remember.

The War with the Weeds

The Philistines are forming fours
Bracken rarake and gorse

> I the Roundhead, Goth, the Hun,
> I the Turk, the Golden Horde,
> The icecap marching, icecap melting,
> I the forearm of the Lord.

In these lists the shivery-grass
Will lose its hundred tidy hearts

Chickweed cocksfoot and fat hen
Will never join their flocks again

    I the first dust of the desert,
    I the blade of flickering light,
    Schoolboy, savage, dairy farmer,
    I the black and final blight.

How convolvulus will writhe
In the incisors of the scythe

And no scarlet pimpernel
Will save the dandelion from hell

KEITH SINCLAIR

Lord of All I Survey

Lord we have not forgotten them, the pioneers,
They did it all for money, saw
On the branches guineas dancing in the flames,
But we do it for love, hope of salvation,
Do we? The laying down of paths,
The shrubs planted, dug up, shifted,
The pruning, the cultivation of the sweet pea.
Two millions of pioneers painting
New shapes on the canvas of a new land,
Boldly moving soil from one side of the section
To the other, two million pioneers. Why,
Why must everyone dig on Sunday morning?

Did the old men do something indiscreet in the darkness,
In the bush, some sin which we must expiate,
Make it right with the soil? Do we all

Look at the hills round our town and say
It must have looked great when grandfather came?
Why do we long to live in a shack in the tea-tree?

Do we perhaps hanker for the great days,
Ashamed of free weekends,—
For Sunday is the devil's day,
Leisure is the entrance fee to sin,—
And so battle with our flesh in the sun,
Lashing our skin with the whips of wind,
Beside the obscenity of the compost heap?

We are owned by gardens, Jews,
Who as we chain them, tax them,
Spit, spit on them from great superior heights,
Heap them with medieval contumely,
Still have the papers mortgaging our castles,
Wives, still hold the passports of our lives.

In every garden there is a singing bird,
Between the beans, beside the corn,
Behind the green and singing grapes,
Sitting in every garden there is a tiger.

Following my mower round the curves I made
Mother I am monarch of all I survey.

KEITH SINCLAIR

from The Ballad of Halfmoon Bay

Edward Edwards was a castaway sealer,
Edward Edwards was a runagate sailor.
He fled from the pressgang or a midland slum,
Slunk from the bilge of a sharp right whaler.

Fed on bully-beef and mutton bird,
Smelling to heaven of his salty board,
He dressed in the slops of the prideless poor,
Walked in the eye of a watchful Lord.

Edwards and his woman lived in sin,
Briding and breeding just the same
And caring for two orphans that seamen left,
Twenty years until the bishop came.

Mary Hinekino was white as a half-caste,
Gentle as the daughter of a Kentish priest.
She spoke the King's English like a currency lass, though
Born to the flavour of a cannibal feast.

Mary and her man had two squeakers to raise—
Throats of conch unless stopped on her breast,
And the sun called them mess-mates, the moon to tea.
Days at the double and at night no rest,

Still she managed and mothered the orphans—
Friday, the foundling, a right tight lad,
The son of a sealing-gang that stayed for a season,
Long in the nose like his unseen dad;

Sarah the other was the moon in the spindrift,
Bright for a lady-love and not sixteen,
As dark as the last light held in a rock pool,
Begotten by her mother for a yard of jean.

Edwards had an island for his back-yard,
Edwards had a whare with a roof of thatch,
A Brown Bess, a go-ashore, a print of the *Savannah*,
Six fat grunters and a small spud patch.

One day he built a cutter on the beach,
Next day worked in his potato patch,
Another he sold fresh victuals to a whaler,
Sometimes he fished in an evening slatch.

Friday and he were the terror of the blue cod.
Where they sailed the groper fled,
From the Land of the Living round to Ruggedy;
Hounded the green-bone past Red Head.

Monday to Saturday he farmed, skinned seal,
Sunday he hoisted his red sprit-sail
And walked his cutter to Halfmoon Bay,
Fair or weather or a two-reef gale.

M. K. JOSEPH

For Any Beachhead

'He lost his life'—yet was the reach
　　Of all his love grasped in that breath;
Upon this battered scrap of beach
　　He 'lost his life'? He found his death.

M. K. JOSEPH

Braque

Marble is veined as leaves and fruit
is sliced ripe into crackleware dishes
bottles can twist a room into their
cool cylinders and knives shine like oil
slicing porcelain fruit into the

suave dishes the light is ripe
and the linen cloth crisp to fingers
on the grained wood and the marble
veined like the leaves in the leaning
tall vase has a shape of jonquils
O glorious the bread is crust and crumb
to be cut by the steel knife with the horn
handle and eaten with pear
and grape and pomegranate
by the smooth light of the marble
the wood the glass the linen the leaves and
all the patterned dark of their shadows.

M. K. JOSEPH

Drunken Gunners

The gunners move like figures in a dance
Harmoniously at their machine that kills
Quite casually beyond the shadowed hills
Under the blue and echoing air of France.
The passing driver watches them askance:
'Look at the beggars—pickled to the gills.'
Yet bodies steadied in parade-ground skills
Correct the tottering mind's intemperance.

Housed under summer leafage at his ease,
Artillery board set up, the captain sees
His rule connect two dots a league apart
And throws destruction at hypotheses,
Wishing that love had ministers like these
To strike its distant enemy to the heart.

Normandy, 1944

M. K. JOSEPH

Victory March

What did you build the trophy of, soldier, soldier?

Of bottles, broken parasols and bones in blackened tanks
Of mud and mines and message-pads, of shells and charabancs
   Of chamber-pots and panzerfaust, of jerricans and jeeps
   Of carrion and crated roads, of rust and rubbish-heaps.

What was your marching music, soldier, soldier?

The sons of morning singing the glory of the Word
Set thunder clouds a-ringing, but all we heard
   Was the tunes of Tinpan Alley from a million radios
   And the wind lamenting where the river flows.

What will be your dream tonight, soldier, soldier?

I shall see children playing in the rubble of a street
And a girl who turned to folly for a tin of meat
   I shall hear an old man weeping by a broken door
   And I shan't sleep so easy as the lads who march no more.

M. K. JOSEPH

Vacation Exercise

In vacant intraterminal hush
Unheeded rings the telephone,
The cleaner with his wire brush
Castigates the grubby stone.

From the empty lecture room
Where board and lectern idly brood
Still echoes distantly the boom
Of the expiring platitude.

Safe from the exploring finger
Pascal and Plato stand at ease.
Eclecticisms drowse and linger
On the shelves of libraries.

Doctor and don have gone their ways
To the mountains and the sands
With mermaids singing roundelays
With satyrs dancing sarabands.

M. K. JOSEPH

Secular Litany

That we may never lack two Sundays in a week
One to rest and one to play
That we may worship in the liturgical drone
Of the race-commentator and the radio raconteur
That we may avoid distinction and exception
Worship the mean, cultivate the mediocre
Live in a state house, raise forcibly-educated children
Receive family benefits, and standard wages and a pension
And rest in peace in a state crematorium
   Saint Allblack
   Saint Monday Raceday
   Saint Stabilisation
     Pray for us.

From all foreigners, with their unintelligible cooking
From the vicious habit of public enjoyment
From kermesse and carnival, high day and festival
From pubs cafés bullfights and barbecues
From Virgil and vintages, fountains and fresco-painting
From afterthought and apperception
From tragedy, from comedy
And from the arrow of God
    Saint Anniversaryday
    Saint Arborday
    Saint Labourday
        Defend us.

When the bottles are empty
And the keg runs sour
And the cinema is shut and darkened
And the radio gone up in smoke
And the sports-ground flooded
When the tote goes broke
And the favourite scratches
And the brass bands are silenced
And the car is rusted by the roadside
    Saint Fathersday
    Saint Mothersday
    Saint Happybirthday
        Have mercy on us.

And for your petitioner, poor little Jim,
    Saint Hocus
    Saint Focus
    Saint Bogus
    And Saint Billy Bungstarter
        Have mercy on him.

M. K. JOSEPH

The New Moses

A pillar of fire went before them by night
  A pillar of cloud by day
But the signpost at the crossroad said
  Hiroshima Ten Miles Away.

When he came down the mountain
  With the tablets in his hand
He found them worshipping the golden calf
  So he stepped in behind the band.

With his staff he struck the rock
  Out the petrol started
Then they moved up the line of trucks
  And with full tanks departed.

He organized a service
  For gathering the quails and manna
So that they could be properly rationed
  And properly taxed. Hosanna!

But when they came to the riverside
  Lord! how their faces fell
The cherub with the fiery sword
  Was waiting there as well.

M. K. JOSEPH

from Mercury Bay Eclogue

Dominus regnavit, exsultet terra: laetentur insulae multae

I

The child's castle crumbles; hot air shimmers
Like water working over the empty sand.
Summer noon is long and the brown swimmers
For fear of outward currents, lie on land.
With tumbleweed and seashells in its hand
The wind walks, a vigorous noonday ghost
Bearing gifts for an expected guest.

Hull down on horizon, island and yacht
Vanish into blue leaving no trace;
Above my head the nebulae retreat
Dizzily sliding round the bend of space
Winking a last red signal of distress.
Each galaxy or archipelago
Plunges away into the sky or sea.

In the dry noon are all things whirling away?
They are whirling away, but look—the gull's flight
Stonefall towards the rainbows of the spray
Skim swim and glide on wing up to the light
And in this airy gesture of delight
See wind and sky transformed to bless and warn
The dance, the transfiguration, the return.

The turning wheels swing the star to harbour
And rock the homing yacht in a deep lull,
Bring children to their tea beneath the arbour,

284

Domesticate the wind's ghost and pull
Islands to anchor, softly drop the gull
Into his nest of burnished stones and lead
The yachtsmen and the swimmers to their bed.

II

A shepherd on a bicycle
Breaks the pose of pastoral
   But will suffice to keep
   The innocence of sheep.

Ringing his bell he drives the flock
From sleepy field and wind-scarred rock
   To where the creaming seas
   Wash shoreward like a fleece.

The farmer and his wife emerge
All golden from the ocean-surge
   Their limbs and children speak
   The legend of the Greek.

The shadowy tents beneath the pines
The surfboards and the fishing-lines
   Tell that our life might be
   One of simplicity.

The wind strums aeolian lyres
Inshore among the telephone wires
   Linking each to each
   The city and the beach.

For sunburnt sleepers would not come
If inland factories did not hum
   And this Arcadian state
   Is built on butterfat.

So children burn the seastained wood
And tell the present as a good
  Knowing that bonfires are
  Important as a star.

And on his gibbet the swordfish raised
With bloody beak and eye glazed
  Glares down into the tide
  Astonishment and pride.

Machine once muscled with delight
He merges now in primitive night;
  The mild and wondering crowd
  Admire the dying god
  Where Kupe and where Cook have trod.

M. K. JOSEPH

Old Montague

(*from The Lovers and the City*)

Summer is sadness and its vivid light
Recalls the stirring of old broils and brawls
Under the glare. How empty are the streets
Surrendered to the intolerable heat
Where no voice troubles all the yellow air
Of the little city held
Secure within the elbow of the river.
The turnspit rusts, the moth the mouse the rat
The spider work their will on plank and cloth
And quiet dust unswept by idle servants
Invades the hall and stairway. The door

Has never closed since the raw morning
When they called me from my wife's deathbed
To my son's deathbed under the dark vault.

My personal light is done. All's dark within
While sunlight hammers on the closed shutters
The house is empty even of its ghosts
Though sometimes I think I see
Two shadows pass before me down the gallery
And a girl's voice singing high in air
Softly mimicked by the mandolin.
(Only the green bucket dripping in the well
Only the cicada on the wall.)

When evening comes I'll take my staff and walk
The orange flambeau weaving before me, through
The violet streets, to Capulet's and the accustomed
Game of chess, which he will always win.

M. K. JOSEPH

On the Mountain

*And if the sufferings of children go to swell the sum of
sufferings which was necessary to pay for truth, then I
protest that the truth is not worth such a price.*—Dostoevski.

The bones of the children cried out upon the mountain
Thin bones, bird bones, crying like birds
Up the glacier birdfooted tracks
Hens' feet crows' feet, old snow old world.

The blood of the children cried out upon pavements
The burnt flesh of children screamed in the cities.
All over the earth machines stopped
Animals were dumb men stood listening
And this terrible crying accused
   The men in gold braid who make wars
   The men in silk hats who make peace
   The men in leather jackets who make revolutions
   The men in frock coats who break revolutions.

Then from His throne spoke the Lord Jehovah
Saying: Bring Me millstones
A mountain of hollow stones for the necks
Of those who offended these My children.
And He was angry, saying: Let there be ocean
Unplumbed depths, bewildering fishes
For each transgressor one halter and one stone.
The angry waves roared *Aaaahhhhh.*

Still the bones of the children cried out
The blood cried from the cobblestones
The paper bones glittering on ice
The honey blood swarming with blue flies.
By the ocean-sea walked the Lord Jehovah
Thinking millenniums; about His feet
Cherubim played ducks and drakes
With the hollow stones. The sea said *Hussshhhh.*

He heard the feet of a million walking
Unhurried, firm, from valley and plain
Before them ran trembling those to be judged
   Flapping and fumbling
   Mouthing and mumbling
   Stooping and stumbling

Over the icy stones
 The men with gold eyes
 The men with silk hands
 The men with leather hearts
 The men with no faces
To be judged: to be brought to judgment
Before the children's bones, on the holy mountain.

RUTH GILBERT

Rachel

Black night without, and blacker night within,
Night we had dreamed both bountiful and wise,
Night that spurned Rachel, smiled on Leah's sin
And willed a blindness on my lover's eyes.

There were no stars, and clouds upon the moon
Darkened the vine-yards; restively astir
Winds cried among the olive-boughs too soon
And Leah spoke, and Jacob answered her . . .

He came in singing, singing from the feast,
Singing our love and the long years fulfilled,
Singing my beauty, and the dark increased
And anguish walked until his song was stilled . . .

My love, my love, had you not wit to guess
Another mouth than mine beneath your own?
Had Leah's hands no alien tenderness,
Her voice no strange, no unfamiliar tone?

I can forgive you everything but this—
Laban and Leah struck no keener blow—
One stole my bridal, one my marriage kiss,
But you were blind, and slept, and did not know.

Li Po

Li Po the poet
(Some called him fool)
Flirted with the moon
In a lacquer pool.

Laughing, tipsy,
Bowed to the water,
Flirting with the young moon
Before he caught her.

Babbling, capering,
Wagging his head—
Only the moon knows
What Li Po said . . .

Li Po was found
(Ah, surely fools are blest!)
Asleep in a lacquer pool,
A young moon on his breast.

RUTH GILBERT

from And There Shall Be No More Death

That which the long scythe whispered to the grass,
And wan leaves, falling, rumoured in the land;
That which bells tolled, and whose first portent was
A dead moth in a child's astonished hand;

That which a bird wrote blackly upon snow;
That which a spent hare scrawled across my path
In a dark wood, I read again, and know
Their lessons' far, but destined aftermath.

All that they strove to teach me, I find true;
Their voices reach me with prophetic din,
Where, in this room, I stand and look on you,
And know you dead, yet cannot take death in.

CHARLES SPEAR

The Watchers

The bulging rampart streaked with pink and jade
Shelters the quay where heedless drinkers sit,
Discoursing love with gin and orangeade,
Or Marcel Proust to a banana split.

The waiters on their monorail recur
Like an old and boring complex; all aglow
The ironclads out at sea fire through the blur
And sink to the rhythms of *El Chocolo*.

CHARLES SPEAR

Karl

All day he stood at Weeping Cross,
While with its shot-ripped flags and battered train,
In full retreat, and stunned by loss,
The army came back through the freezing rain.

Behind, the rearguard seemed to swirl and drown,
As the gunsmoke curdled through the pass.
The slamming volleys switched the wet leaves down,
And scythed the dead upon the reddened grass.

Have done! Let none hereafter heed this cry
For the apostolic chivalry of time long past;
This prayer of all that smote the marble sky
Is least, and yet the proudest, for it is the last.

CHARLES SPEAR

Christoph

The wind blew strongly like the voice of fate
Through cheerless sunlight, and the black yawl strained
And creaked across the sullen slate
Of Zuider Zee. That night it rained;

The Hook of Holland drenched in diamonds lay
Far southward; but the exile coming home
Turns back to hours like golden tissues stacked away,
And sees no more the sulky, weltering foam,
But only roses, or white honey in the comb.

CHARLES SPEAR

1894 in London

Like torn-up newsprint the nonchalant snow
Creaked down incessantly on Red Lion Square.
Clock chimes were deadbeats. Clang! Nowhere to go!
The cabbies drove with marble stare,
The snowed-up statues had a pensive air.

Inside the pub the spirits flowed,
And Sal and Kate the guardees' tanners shared;
Out in the dusk the newsboys crowed,
And to infinity the lamp-posts flared,
The gas-blue lilies of the Old Kent Road.

Old England's blue hour of unmeasured nips,
The Quiet Time for Dorian Gray,
The day off for the barmaid's hips,
Prayer-Book revision time down Lambeth way.

CHARLES SPEAR

Die Pelzaffen

By flowers of china-pink and lily pads
Metallic with the burnish of the sun,
Beneath a sky of lint, the village lads
Run out and cheer for holidays begun;
And decades later out again they run.

It is the long frontier; the cossacks ride
And smoke and swing their curling whips;
The boys peer from the German side
Like bergamasks with grinning lips.

'Fur apes,' they jeer, 'you showed your heels
At Balaklava. Cowards!' Snakelike they slip
Beneath the boughs; the shaggy rider wheels
And swears and brings the carbine to his hip.

Shaken as leaves in a great wind,
Across the cramping glass again they swerve
Into the convex, and their voices thinned
Entwine like harp notes on time's weltering curve.

The Anchorage

Fifteen or twenty feet below,
The little fish come creeping round the anchor chain.
I could not have it quieter now,
Not anywhere, nor could there be less movement
Anywhere at all than here.

The bay moves on into night.
The shadows come to watch and wait in every hollow
Till they have gathered-in all.
But moon comes over the rocks; she lights the little fall
And rise and fall at the beach.

Deep water, deep bay
So still and calm for one whole night in the south-east
That day has never come,
And I am still upon my knees out on the stern,
And you and I still watch
Down twenty, thirty feet below.

Cuvier Light

Perennial fluctuation,
Interior lift of the sea,
Mist or a light rain, and silence—

Suppose our breathing is this movement,
This mist, our wishes coming back to us,
The rain, some forgiveness of our rashness,
The night, all that is against us—

Land all along one side,
One lamp turned low in the cabin,
Two lights to sea and then great Cuvier,

Admirable light!
Swinging, like a discus
On the arm of its taut brilliant beam,
The whole massed weight of the night!

PAT WILSON

The Precious Pearl

The oyster shuts his gates to form the pearl.
He knows he has a saviour caught within him,
Poor fool, old Oyster. And it works against him,
An irritant that's locked within his shell,
A single-mindedness that thins his heart,
Turns it to narrow-heartedness. Yet he,
Poor foolish oyster, used to love the sea
In all its many forms, to every part
Open with tranquil, unassuming jaws.
Then that foul irritant was driven in,
And snap! the wounded tongue cherished its sin
Until at last by hard, immobile laws
    A shining, perfect pebble made from wrong—
    A perfect grievance—rolled from off the tongue.

PAT WILSON

The Tree

The day the big tree went
There came two rather seedy-looking men
Full of the mysteries of their craft.
They spoke loudly yet confidentially to each other,
Nodded to me and my brother,
Said good morning to my brother's wife,
Cleared away all the little children of the neighbourhood,
And addressed themselves
To their big, supple saw.

Two or three hours later under the tree
They were still only half-way through.
The cut had a tell-tale concave scoop
Where each had been pulling down at the end of his stroke.
There was much previous talk of wedges,
Much arranging of ropes,
Calculation of angles,
And my brother and I were taking turns at the saw.

And so we all got friendly there with each other,
Putting the mysteries away
Under the great macrocarpa tree.
And when it started to lift and heave
And when the earth shook and the great sigh went up
As it fell and settled,
Then all the birds came flying out in a cloud
And all the children flew in with shouts and cries
And started a battle with the cones
And made their huts and houses in the fir.

PAT WILSON

The Farewell

And so, one day when the tide was away out,
The gulls there dancing along the edge of the sea,
We walked across the sand, down to the boat
And began again—she to protest and appeal,
I to refuse, looking aside, and then turning
And smiling . . .
                    for it was not as if I had
Whatever it was that she asked, but who could persuade her
Of that? nor was it true that I could pretend
For ever . . .
                    and all the gulls there, crying and playing,
Hunting, and all the reds and browns and yellows
Of late afternoon, and the last tints of the blue
Going out with the tide, and the boat drawn up there fast
Becoming high and dry on the sand as we talked.

PAT WILSON

The Childhood Church

The town was full of bells, where I grew up—
No sound seems quite so peaceful now as theirs,
Nothing is quite so peaceful as those bells
Suiting the Sunday air and summer evenings,
Church-bells by the end of any street
And along the green borders of the town,
The flowers and small trees lining the avenues.

297

But if I feel this now, it is because
It was so then. I was not sent to church,
Nor belonged to any Sunday School,
And had no business with the Maori church—
Maoris were strange and quite unknowable
Straggling in, in twos and threes, to town
Over the railway bridge—and now, these bells
Bear not the sound of churches but of childhood.

Such curious bells—the bell from the other side
Across the harbour where the Maoris lived
Around behind the point: going past
In the launch or sailing, we would look
So carefully at the church, trying to see,
To make quite certain that it really owned
The bell we heard, for Maoris surely lived
Some other place as well—this place like an outpost—
Somewhere quite hidden and perhaps quite alien,
As its people, part of an earlier world—
Yet friendly in the bell's ringing on Sundays,
Clear, monotonous across the harbour
So that we stopped and said, 'That's the Maori church,'
And stayed and listened to its curious chime.

And then, just down the road, the English church
Was hidden too, save for its red tin roof,
Hidden by wealthy, precious trees at the front,
Pohutukawas, hedged-in by hydrangeas
And, by the footpath, one huge clump of bamboo—
Cut down two years ago but, until then,
Always rustling, alive and shaking with sparrows.
There was the Catholic church with its long flight
Of concrete steps and two great, rough, dark trees

Hanging above, and a schoolroom near. And, too,
A Methodist, down one small avenue . . .
A town of churches, and a town of bells
But all impalpable and sourceless chimes,
Sometimes guessed-at in passing, never found.

How could I speak as gently as their sound?
As gently, and yet as insistently
So that one lay and listened after dark
And there was a kind of terror in their warmth
And yet a kind of comfort as they tolled,
The Sunday bells tolling and turning within
The welcome space of evening and of rest.
They did not ring from churches, for I loved
And knew no church. They rang for no good cause,
No reason that I knew, but as a gift
From a wider church than those beside the streets,
Something of places and names, not of churches,
Though church-bells must have been its symbol then.

COLIN NEWBURY

Letter from Paparua

A letter today, official, buff,
Stamped with the Service of the King,
From one to whom kings were a bluff,
Nobility a clay, and estate a pall
To hide the corruption of us all.

Which led him unthinking to express
His needs in common acquisition,
To barter, filch, and sometimes undress
In backrooms, less from love of sin
Than from a sense of hopelessness.

Thus for the public protection
He inhabits fifteen feet of the State,
And for a treat weeds flower-beds in the sun;
And in this letter tortures his thought
Into an apology for the great untaught.

Yet I have seen him stride
Through morning mist to the byre
Singing out his soul to the herd
Stumbling to his call down the paddock mire,
Deliver a foal, mend a bird.

And keep somewhere behind his eyes
A respect for country law,
A happy inarticulate surprise
At the wisdom of the seasons' turning,
Till a weak will began his unlearning.

COLIN NEWBURY

New Wine, Old Bottles

They had known it all before, routine
Romance, comedy in clandestine:
Tinkle of chatter and tea-cups after the show,
Confessional titbits, mutual dislikes,
Books, records, films, the radio;

Wire-lifting gallantry on Saturday hikes;
A blown fuse, lost torch,
First tremulous kiss on the midnight porch.

They had heard it all before: accusations,
The tedious half-truths of explanations;
And then the letters—white leaves
Drifting under the door unseen—
By autumn, fewer: their minds, like trees,
Had shaken themselves clean,
And they accepted as natural law,
Winter wind in the heart, the closed door.

But this was new: years after,
When time had fractured their laughter,
When blood flowed thicker in the vein,
Mind, walking at her summer ease
In step with heart in evergreen,
Threw off her coat of frieze,
Danced a step or two to meet
Heart's old folly ambling up the street.

And so, for convenience, they were married.
(Just as companions, the neighbours said.)
How could he, in the gentle guise
Of respectable middle-aged affection,
Tie down truths with half-lies,
Hide heart's old intention?
Yet found, knocking at her door,
No answer; this, at least, was as before.

COLIN NEWBURY

The Epilogue of the Wandering Jew

And that is all I really have to say. Looking
Around, I see you are like the others wherever I have spoken:
    Your pride is ruffled; you look crestfallen;
    And some of you at the back are weeping.

I have not told you everything I have seen;
You could not bear that. For I have learned
    To be, shall we say, careful in front of children;
    And no longer prophesy, (I do not like being stoned.)

How your questions rushed upon me like a flock of birds
At an old fruit tree, shrilling with excitement
    Flailing my years to gobble words.
    And for novelties, curios, eager as turbulent

Urchins, you gathered round Isaac peddler come to town
With a pack-full of history. And for a while I let you play
    With some pretty court scandals of far-away
    Rulers, ruled by Madam or the Clown.

Yet, when I unravelled, (but only because you pressed me,)
Some local haberdashery, you were quarrelsome and swore
    The new-spun stuff the same devilry
    And dice that I had shown you before.

Then the Worthies came forward, much obsessed by Fact,
With queries of When and Where; (sorry Reverend,
    But the Sermon meant what it says; like my friend
    Paul, I cannot distinguish truth from tact.)

Perhaps I do not understand your learned pretension
To see Future and Past. I, being in the tents of Israel,
   Or on your boulevard, equally Here, fail
    To remember that Elsewhere is your preoccupation.

For my Time is not your Time that burns your hours to
 embers.
I walk a plain; you a blazing corridor with your eyes
   On nothing, or behind on the charred timbers,
    Peering into the ashes of razed cities

For a few bones, a tablet—some proof of your identity.
You grope the narrow way; I behold the sphere,
   And do not need a map to know that we are every-
    where
    With good or ill, whatever the country.

Thus you will have learned from me what you already knew:
(Hence your disappointment,) that a kingdom dies
   Through abuse of the potter's wheel; and a few
    Careful hands have moulded dynasties.

Let this suffice you, and the certainty of your birth;
No more. Be excellent as the potter, and loving
   With the hands, before your faltering
    Is consumed in the flame and shadow of Death.

For I am reminded He is the one I seek
Among you: Caliban of the young—the old man's familiar
   Attendant; and you do Him wrong to speak
    Of Him behind His back in a whisper.

He is no slave—though I have seen Him serve your turn—
But like the good servant, knows his cue well. . . .
   But you shrink, and for all my answers will not tell
    Me the only Answer you and not I can learn.

So be it then. Maybe your children's children will show
Me how to look unflinching into the eye of your Companion.
Or they will be sand as you; and I, a shadow
Upon them, ever lengthening in the sun.

MARY STANLEY

Record Perpetual Loss

Automaton whose stiffened gesture writes
footnotes to faces, none escapes your hand.
A finger irresponsible as wind
or water smoothes away all feature from
the loved image at last anonymous.
Lighter than dust the remembered kiss is lost
forever on the lip of chance. By change
the migratory heart is turned to fresh
preoccupations; hour by hour, act
by act, this counterpoint of breath removes
the past, empties the echo from the ear.
What mirror or wintry crystal may record
perpetual loss, by separation chafe
my eye to tears? This *I*, I was, is not
older only by years, rejects the girl
I would not recognise whose fictions grown
too thin with use are useless to refute
the cold unanswerable logic of a death.

MARY STANLEY

The Wife Speaks

Being a woman, I am
not more than man nor less
but answer imperatives
of shape and growth. The bone
attests the girl with dolls,
grown up to know the moon
unwind her tides to chafe
the heart. A house designs
my day an artifact
of care to set the hands
of clocks, and hours are round
with asking eyes. Night puts
an ear on silence where
a child may cry. I close
my books and know events
are people, and all roads
everywhere walk home
women and men, to take
history under their roofs.
I see Icarus fall
out of the sky, beside
my door, not beautiful,
envy of angels, but feathered
for a bloody death.

MARY STANLEY

Per Diem et per Noctem

Birds in their oratory of leaves
Clamour at morning over my love.
All waters praise him, the sea harbours
from harm, all islands are his neighbour
and rain at daybreak feathers his peace
softer than pillows or my kiss.

O may his lucky hand at noon
pluck down the sun, all day his keen
eye be darkened by no cloud.
Sky-walker, the lonely hawk, applaud
his purpose, the equipoise among
cliff and rock, his difficult song.

O never may night confound or send
him lost into that hinterland
far from my coasts. Where is your moon,
Endymion, trimming her thin
flame to light my love? The world
lifts its shoulder to shelter him curled
in the lap of sleep. By falling star
I wish all his tomorrows fair.

THE SOURCES OF THE POEMS

It will be of interest to the reader tracing the development of New Zealand poetry to know when and where poems were first published. Accordingly, we have listed as compactly as possible the periodical or book in which, so far as we have been able to discover, each poem made its first appearance. Figures in parentheses refer to the numbers given to the poems in the list of Contents. Since New Zealand is without a bibliography of its poetry we have also listed the works of the poets included here.

* Anthology   † Joint production

JACOBS   (1)   *The Lyttelton Times*, 14 Jan. 1854, p. 10.

BARR   (2–6)   *Poems and Songs*, 1861, pp. 62, 71, 131, 144, 226.

DOMETT   (7–13)   *Ranolf and Amohia*, 1872, pp. 79, 90, 230, 232, 235, 265, 301.

BROOME   (14)   **Canterbury Rhymes*, 1883, p. 108.

MACKAY   (15)   *The Sitter on the Rail; and Other Poems*, 1891, p. 19. (16) **New Zealand Verse*, 1906, p. 17. (17) *From the Maori Sea*, [1908], p. 23. (18) *The Bride of the Rivers, and Other Verses*, 1926, p. 37.

REEVES   (19) †*In Double Harness*, 1891, p. 77. (20–22) *New Zealand and Other Poems*, 1898, pp. 4, 21, 44. (23) **New Zealand Verse*, 1906, p. 22.

WRIGHT   (24–27) *Station Ballads and Other Verses*, 1897, pp. 16, 55, 70, 99. (28) *Wisps of Tussock*, 1900, p. 54.

CHURCH   (29–30) *The West Wind*, 1902, pp. 13, 15. (31) *Poems*, [1904], p. 4. (32) *Poems*, 1912, p. 142.

BAUGHAN   (33–35) *Reuben and Other Poems*, 1903, pp. 75, 87, 90.

ROGERS   (36–37)   *The Bulletin*, 18 Aug. 1904, p. 3; 8 June 1905, p. 3.

STENHOUSE   (38)   *Lays from Maoriland*, 1908, p. 24.

MANSFIELD   (39–40)   *Poems*, 1923, pp. 46, 47.

MASON   (41)   *The Chapbook (A Miscellany)*, (London), no. 39, [Oct.?], 1924, p. 29.   (42–43)   *The Beggar*, 1924, pp. 5, 15.   (44)   *Penny Broadsheet*, 1925.   (45)   *Phoenix*, vol. 2, no. 2, June 1933, p. 17.   (46–51)   *No New Thing*, 1934, pp. 4, 5, 6, 7, 8, 17.   (52)   *End of Day*, 1936, poem 1.

ROSS   (53)   *Stars in the Mist*, 1928, p. 91.

CRESSWELL   (54)   *Poems (1921–27)*, 1928, p. 40.   (55–56)   *Poems (1924–31)*, 1931, pp. 24, 52.   (57–59)   *Lyttelton Harbour*, 1936, pp. 8, 33, 38.

BETHELL   (60–62)   *From a Garden in the Antipodes*, 1929, pp. 9, 15, 18.   (63)   *Time and Place*, 1936, p. 12.   (64)   *Day and Night, Poems 1924–1935*, 1939, p. 4.   (65)   *Collected Poems*, 1950, p. 94.

DUGGAN   (66)   *New Zealand Best Poems of 1933*, p. 8.   (67)   *New Zealand Best Poems of 1934*, p. 11.   (68–69)   *Poems*, 1937, pp. 27, 43.   (70–72)   *More Poems*, 1951, pp. 13, 54, 64.

BEAGLEHOLE   (73)   *Art in New Zealand*, no. 20, June 1933, p. 213.

FAIRBURN   (74)   *New Poems*, July 1934, p. 30.   (75) †*Another Argo*, Aug. 1935.   (76)   *Dominion*, March 1938, p. 11.   (77–80)   †*Recent Poems*, Feb. 1941, pp. 45, 46, 48, 49.   (81)   *Book 6*, Sept. 1942, p. 5.   (82–83)   *Poems 1929–41*, Feb. 1943, pp. 18, 28.   (84)   *The Rakehelly Man*, 1946, p. 30.   (85)   *Arts Year Book*, 1947, p. 155.   (86)   *Arts Year Book*, 1950, p. 142.   (87)   *Three Poems*, 1952, p. 55.   (88)   *Poetry Yearbook*, 1952, p. 30.

HYDE   (89)   *New Zealand Best Poems of 1934*, p. 15.   (90)   *Art in New Zealand*, no. 29, Sept. 1935, p. 30.   (91–99)

HYDE—*cont.*

    Houses by the Sea, 1952, pp. 109, 116, 117, 118, 121, 122, 125, 125, 127. (100) *Art in New Zealand*, no. 42, Dec. 1938, p. 74. (101) *Art in New Zealand*, no. 50, Dec. 1940, p. 89.

STEWART (102) *New Zealand Best Poems of 1935*, p. 22. (103) *Green Lions*, [1937], p. 11.

GLOVER (104) **Verse Alive*, March 1936, p. 25. (105) †*Recent Poems*, Feb. 1941, p. 36. (106) *Book 3*, Aug. 1941, p. 10. (107–108) *The Wind and the Sand, Poems 1934-44*, 1945, pp. 12, 40. (109–110) *New Zealand Listener*, 28 May 1948; 30 June 1950. (111–112) *Arts Year Book*, 1950, both at p. 130. (113) *Poetry Yearbook*, 1951, p. 33. (114) *Arts Year Book*, 1951, p. 108. (115) *Arawata Bill*, 1953, p. 23. (116–117) †*Recent Poems*, Feb. 1941, pp. 31, 32. (118) *Book 8*, Aug. 1946, p. 50. (119) *Book 7*, Feb. 1946, p. 28. (120) *Arts Year Book*, 1946, p. 122. (121) *The Arts in New Zealand*, no. 68, June-July 1945, p. 9. (122) *Sings Harry*, 1951, p. 16. (123) *Landfall* 6, June 1948, p. 120.

CURNOW (124–125) *Not in Narrow Seas*, March 1939, poems 1, 6. (126–130) †*Recent Poems*, Feb. 1941, pp. 10, 12, 13, 15, 17. (131–132) *Island and Time*, March 1941, pp. 20, 31. (133) *Book 1*, March 1941, p. 13. (134) †*Abel Janszoon Tasman and the Discovery of New Zealand*, 1942, p. 7. (135) *Poetry* (Chicago), vol. 63, no. 2, Nov. 1943, p. 75. (136) *Sailing or Drowning*, [1943?], p. 9. (137) *The Arts in New Zealand*, no. 67, April-May 1945, p. 30. (138) *Landfall* 13, March 1950, p. 42.

BRASCH (139) *The Land and the People*, 1939, p. 29. (140) *Book 4*, Sept. 1941, p. 7. (141) *Book 5*, Feb. 1942, p. 13. (142–145) *Disputed Ground*, April 1948, pp. 18, 24, 39, 47. (146–147) First publication.

HERVEY   (148) *Book 2*, May 1941, p. 14. (149) *Book 4*, Sept.
1941, p. 4. (150–151) *New Poems*, 1942, pp. 11, 22.
(152) *Poetry, a Quarterly of Australian and New Zealand
Verse*, no. 9, [Dec. 1943], p. 4. (153) *Man on a Raft and
Other Poems*, July 1949, p. 23. (154–155) *New Zealand
Listener*, 1 July 1949; 5 Dec. 1952. (156) *She Was My
Spring*, 1955, p. 10.

DOWLING   (157) *A Day's Journey*, 1941, p. 20. (158) *Signs
and Wonders*, 1944, p. 27. (159) *The Arts in New Zea-
land*, no. 69, Sept.-Oct. 1945, p. 12. (160) *Arts Year
Book*, 1946, p. 118. (161) *Book 9*, July 1947, p. 40. (162)
Arts Year Book, 1948, p. 151. (163) *Canterbury and Other
Poems*, 1949, p. 16. (164) *Landfall* 22, June 1952, p. 144.

VOGT   (165) *Poems for a War*, 1943, p. 30. (166) *Poetry
Yearbook*, 1951, p. 62.

WITHEFORD   (167) *New Zealand New Writing*, no. 2,
[1943?], p. 48. (168) *Hilltop*, no. 3, Sept. 1949, p. 17.
(169–170) *Shadow of the Flame*, March 1950, pp. 18, 32.
(171) *Landfall* 24, Dec. 1952, p. 302.

SMITHYMAN   (172) *New Zealand New Writing*, no. 3, June
1944, p. 19. (173) *Seven Sonnets*, 1946, sonnet 6. (174)
Landfall 8, Dec. 1948, p. 267. (175) *New Zealand
Listener*, 12 Aug. 1949. (176–178) First publication.
(179) *Arts Year Book*, 1950, p. 142. (180) *Arena*, no. 39,
1954, p. 14. (181) *The Outlook*, 16 June 1953, p. 10.
(182) First publication. (183) *Landfall* 26, June 1953,
p. 99. (184–185) First publication.

BERTRAM   (186) *Book 8*, Aug. 1946, p. 9. (187) *Spike*, 1947,
p. 22.

JOHNSON   (188–189) *Arena*, no. 16, July 1947, both at p. 5.
(190) *Landfall* 8, Dec. 1948, p. 251. (191) *The Sun
Among the Ruins*, May 1951, p. 20. (192) *Verse 1951*, p.
23. (193) *Roughshod Among the Lilies*, [Dec. 1951], p. 18.

JOHNSON—*cont.*

(194) †*Poems Unpleasant*, 1952, p. 29. (195–196) *Numbers*, no. 1, July 1954, pp. 14, 15.

DALLAS (197) *Landfall* 3, Sept. 1947, p. 186. (198) *New Zealand Listener*, 21 Nov. 1947. (199) *Arts Year Book*, 1949, p. 133. (200) *Landfall* 12, Dec. 1949, p. 305. (201) *Poetry Yearbook*, 1952, p. 24.

OLIVER (202) *Landfall* 4, Dec. 1947, p. 247. (203) *Landfall* 8, Dec. 1948, p. 255. (204–205) *New Zealand Listener*, 11 Nov. 1949; 6 April 1951.

HART-SMITH (206) *Landfall* 6, June 1948, p. 117. (207) *The Wooden Horse*, vol. 1, no. 2, 1950, p. 19. (208) *On the Level*, 1950, p. 31. (209) *Poetry Yearbook*, 1952, p. 38.

BAXTER (210–212) *Blow, Wind of Fruitfulness*, 1948, pp. 15, 20, 48. (213) *Kiwi*, 1948, p. 23. (214) *Canterbury University College Review*, 1948, p. 4. (215–217) *Landfall* 13, March 1950, pp. 8, 10, 12. (218) *Arts Year Book*, 1950, p. 124. (219) *Gaudeamus*, no. 2, May 1951, p. 6. (220–226) *Landfall* 18, June 1951, pp. 92, 95, 96, 97, 99, 99, 102. (227) *Ako-Pai*, 1951, p. 10. (228–229) †*Poems Unpleasant*, 1952, pp. 12, 19. (230) *Landfall* 26, June 1953, p. 114.

CAMPBELL (231) *Spike*, 1948, p. 21. (232) *Hilltop*, no. 2, June 1949, p. 15. (233–234) *Landfall* 11, Sept. 1949, pp. 224, 225. (235–237) *Mine Eyes Dazzle*, June 1950, pp. 27, 32, 35.

SINCLAIR (238) *Landfall* 8, Dec. 1948, p. 262. (239) *Arts Year Book*, 1951, p. 106. (240) *Jindyworobak Anthology 1951*, Feb. 1952, p. 18. (241–242) *Songs for a Summer*, 1952, pp. 16, 18. (243–244) First publication. (245) *Landfall* 27, Sept. 1953, p. 173.

JOSEPH (246) *Arts Year Book*, 1948, p. 160. (247) *Landfall* 14, June 1950, p. 123. (248–252) *Imaginary Islands*,

JOSEPH—*cont.*

[Dec. 1950], pp. 7, 12, 22, 25, 26. (253) *Landfall 24,* Dec. 1952, p. 283. (254) *Landfall* 27, Sept. 1953, p. 171. (255) *Poetry Yearbook,* 1953, p. 86.

GILBERT (256) *New Zealand Listener,* 11 Nov. 1949. (257) *Lazarus and Other Poems,* Nov. 1949, p. 14. (258) *Arts Year Book,* 1951, p. 113.

SPEAR (259) *Arts Year Book,* 1949, p. 142. (260–261) *Arachne,* no. 1, Jan. 1950, pp. 3, 4. (262) *Canta,* 20 Sept. 1950, p. 3. (263) *Gaudeamus,* no. 1, April 1951, p. 3.

WILSON (264) *Landfall* 17, March 1951, p. 20. (265) *Gaudeamus,* no. 2, May 1951, p. 7. (266) *Gaudeamus,* no. 5, Oct. 1951, p. 11. (267) *Poetry Yearbook,* 1951, p. 80. (268–269) *The Bright Sea,* [1951], pp. 8, 26.

NEWBURY (270) *Gaudeamus,* no. 5, Oct. 1951, p. 7. (271) *New Zealand Listener,* 2 Oct. 1953. (272) First publication.

STANLEY (273–275) *Starveling Year,* 1953, pp. 12, 20, 19.

BIBLIOGRAPHY

* Represents a verse play or script.

N.B.—This bibliography does not include the prose works of the authors.

BARR, John of Craigielee:
> *Poems and Songs*, Edinburgh, 1861, W. P. Nimmo; enlarged edn., 1874.
> *Poems*, Dunedin, N.D. (1874), F. Humffray.

BAUGHAN, Blanche Edith:
> *Verses*, London, 1898, Constable.
> *Reuben and Other Poems*, Westminster, 1903, Constable.
> *Shingle-Short*, Christchurch, N.D. (1908), Whitcombe & Tombs.
> *Hope: a Poem*, Christchurch, N.D. (*c.* 1916).
> *Poems From The Port Hills*, Auckland, N.D. (1923), Whitcombe & Tombs.

BAXTER, James Keir:
> *Beyond the Palisade*, Christchurch, 1944, Caxton.
> *Blow, Wind of Fruitfulness*, Christchurch, 1948, Caxton.
> *The Fallen House*, Christchurch, 1953, Caxton.

BEAGLEHOLE, John Cawte:
> *Words for Music*, Christchurch 1938, Caxton.

BETHELL, Mary Ursula ('Evelyn Hayes'):
> *The Haunted Gallery and Other Poems*, London, N.D., Arthur H. Stockwell.
> *The Glad Returning and Other Poems*, London, N.D., Arthur H. Stockwell.
> *From a Garden in the Antipodes*, London, 1929, Sidgwick & Jackson.

BETHELL—*cont.*

Time and Place, Christchurch, 1936, Caxton.

Day and Night, Poems 1924–1935, Christchurch, 1939, Caxton.

Collected Poems, Christchurch, 1950, Caxton.

BRASCH, Charles Orwell:

The Land and the People and Other Poems, Christchurch, 1939, Caxton.

* *The Quest*, London, 1946, The Compass Players.

Disputed Ground, Poems 1939–45, Christchurch, 1948, Caxton.

BROOME, Sir Frederick Napier:

Poems from New Zealand, London, 1868, Houlston & Wright.

The Stranger from Seriphos, London, 1869, Macmillan.

CAMPBELL, Alistair:

Mine Eyes Dazzle, Poems 1947–49, Christchurch, 1950, Pegasus. Another, somewhat altered edn., Christchurch, 1951, Pegasus.

CHURCH, Hubert Newman Wigmore:

The West Wind, Sydney, 1902, *The Bulletin.*

Poems, Wellington, N.D. (1904), Whitcombe & Tombs.

Egmont, Melbourne, 1908, T. C. Lothian.

Poems, Melbourne, 1912, T. C. Lothian.

CRESSWELL, Walter D'Arcy:

Poems (1921–1927), London, 1928, Wells Gardner, Darton.

Poems (1924–1931), N.P., N.D., John Lane The Bodley Head.

Lyttelton Harbour: A Poem, Auckland, 1936, Unicorn.

* *The Forest*, Auckland, 1952, Pelorus.

CURNOW, Thomas Allen Monro:

Valley of Decision (Phoenix Miscellany: 1), Auckland, 1933, Auckland University College Students' Association Press.

CURNOW—*cont.*

Three Poems, Christchurch, 1935, Caxton Club.

Enemies, Poems, 1934–36, Christchurch, 1937, Caxton.

Not In Narrow Seas, Christchurch, 1939, Caxton.

Island and Time, Christchurch, 1941, Caxton.

Sailing Or Drowning, Wellington, N.D. (1943), Progressive.

Jack Without Magic, Christchurch, 1946, Caxton.

At Dead Low Water, Christchurch, 1949, Caxton.

* *The Axe*, Christchurch, 1949, Caxton.

DALLAS, Ruth:

Country Road and Other Poems, 1947–52, Christchurch, 1953, Caxton.

DOMETT, Alfred:

Poems, London, 1833, H. Leggatt.

Venice, London, 1839, Saunders & Otley.

Ranolf and Amohia, London 1872, Smith, Elder.

Revised 2 vol. edn., London, 1883, Kegan Paul, Trench.

Rhymes Old and New, London, 1877, Smith, Elder.

DOWLING, Basil:

A Day's Journey, Christchurch, 1941, Caxton.

Signs And Wonders, Christchurch, 1944, Caxton.

Canterbury and Other Poems, Christchurch, 1949, Caxton.

DUGGAN, Eileen:

Poems, Dunedin, N.D. (1920), *N.Z. Tablet*.

New Zealand Bird Songs, Wellington, 1929, H. H. Tombs.

Poems, London, 1937, Allen & Unwin.

New Zealand Poems, London, 1940, Allen & Unwin.

More Poems, London, 1951, Allen & Unwin.

FAIRBURN, Arthur Rex Dugard:

He Shall Not Rise, London, 1930, Columbia Press.

Dominion, Christchurch, 1938, Caxton.

Poems 1929–1941, Christchurch, 1943, Caxton.

FAIRBURN—*cont.*

The Rakehelly Man, Christchurch, 1946, Caxton.

Three Poems, Wellington, 1952, N.Z. University Press.

Strange Rendezvous, Christchurch, 1952, Caxton.

GILBERT, Ruth:

Lazarus and Other Poems, Wellington, 1949, H. H. Tombs.

GLOVER, Denis:

Thistledown, Christchurch, 1935, Caxton Club.

A Short Reflection On The Present State Of Literature In This Country, Christchurch, 1935, Caxton Club.

Six Easy Ways of Dodging Debt Collectors, Christchurch, 1936, Caxton.

The Arraignment of Paris, Christchurch, 1937, Caxton.

Thirteen Poems, Christchurch, 1939, Caxton.

Cold Tongue, Christchurch, 1940, Caxton.

The Wind and the Sand, Poems, 1934–44, Christchurch, 1945, Caxton.

Summer Flowers, Christchurch, 1946, Caxton.

Sings Harry and Other Poems, Christchurch, 1951, Caxton.

Arawata Bill: A Sequence of Poems, Christchurch, 1953, Pegasus.

HART-SMITH, William:

Columbus Goes West, Adelaide, 1943, Jindyworobak.

Harvest, Melbourne, 1945, Georgian House.

The Unceasing Ground, Sydney, 1946, Angus & Robertson.

Christopher Columbus, Christchurch, 1948, Caxton.

On the Level, Timaru, 1950, the author.

HERVEY, John Russell:

Selected Poems, Christchurch, 1940, Caxton.

New Poems, Christchurch, 1942, Caxton.

Man On a Raft, and Other Poems, Christchurch, 1949, Caxton.

She Was My Spring, Christchurch, 1955, Caxton.

'HYDE, Robin' (Iris Wilkinson):

The Desolate Star, Christchurch, 1929, Whitcombe & Tombs.

The Conquerors, London, 1935, Macmillan.

Persephone in Winter, London, 1937, Hurst & Blackett.

Houses By the Sea and the Later Poems, Christchurch, 1952, Caxton.

JACOBS, Henry:

Shadows of the Old Church, Christchurch, 1870, the author.

A Lay of the Southern Cross, London and Christchurch, 1893, Skeffington.

JOHNSON, Louis:

Stanza and Scene, Wellington, 1945, Handcraft.

The Sun Among the Ruins, Christchurch, 1951, Pegasus.

Roughshod Among the Lilies, Christchurch, 1951, Pegasus.

JOSEPH, Michael Kennedy:

Imaginary Islands, N.P. (Auckland), N.D. (1950), the author.

MACKAY, Jessie:

The Spirit of the Rangatira, Melbourne, 1889, Geo. Robertson.

The Sitter on the Rail; and Other Poems, Christchurch, 1891, Simpson & Williams.

From the Maori Sea, Christchurch, N.D. (1908), Whitcombe & Tombs.

Land of the Morning, Christchurch, N.D. (1909), Whitcombe & Tombs.

Poems of Jessie Mackay, Melbourne, 1911, T. C. Lothian.

The Bride of the Rivers, and Other Verses, Christchurch, 1926, Simpson & Williams.

Vigil, Auckland, N.D. (1935), Whitcombe & Tombs.

'MANSFIELD, Katherine' (Kathleen Beauchamp; Mrs. Middleton Murry):

Poems, London, 1923, Constable.

317

MASON, Ronald Arthur Kels:

>*In the Manner of Men*, Auckland, 1923, the author.
>
>*The Beggar*, Auckland, 1924, the author.
>
>*Penny Broadsheet*, Auckland, 1925, the author.
>
>*No New Thing, Poems 1924–29*, N.P. (Auckland), 1934, Spearhead.
>
>*End of Day*, Christchurch, 1936, Caxton.
>
>* *Squire Speaks*, Auckland, 1938, Caxton.
>
>*This Dark Will Lighten, Selected Poems 1923–41*, Christchurch, 1941, Caxton.
>
>* *China*, N.P. (Auckland), N.D. (1943).

REEVES, William Pember:

>*Colonial Couplets*, (with G. P. Williams), Christchurch, 1889, Simpson & Williams.
>
>*In Double Harness*, (with G. P. Williams), Christchurch, 1891, *Lyttelton Times* Publishing Co.
>
>*New Zealand and Other Poems*, London, 1898, Grant Richards.
>
>*The Passing of the Forest and Other Verse*, London, 1925, the author.

ROSS, David MacDonald:

>*The Afterglow*, Auckland, N.D. (1904), Wilson & Horton.
>
>*The Promise of the Star*, London, N.D. (1906), Jarrold.
>
>*Hearts of the Pure*, Melbourne, 1911, T. C. Lothian.
>
>*Morning Red*, Auckland, 1916, Wildman & Airey.
>
>*Stars in the Mist*, London, 1928, Selwyn & Blount.

SINCLAIR, Keith:

>*Songs for a Summer*, Christchurch, 1952, Pegasus.
>
>*Strangers or Beasts*, Christchurch, 1954, Caxton.

SMITHYMAN, Kendrick:

>*Seven Sonnets*, Auckland, 1946, Pelorus.
>
>*The Blind Mountain*, Christchurch, 1950, Caxton.

SPEAR, Charles:

>*Twopence Coloured*, Christchurch, 1951, Caxton.

STANLEY, Mary (Mrs. K. Smithyman):
Starveling Year, Christchurch, 1953, Pegasus.
STENHOUSE, William MacStravick:
Poems, Songs, and Sonnets, Glasgow, 1886, A. Stenhouse.
Lays from Maoriland, Paisley, 1908, A. Gardner.
STEWART, Douglas:
Green Lions, Auckland, N.D. (1937), the author.
The White Cry, London, 1939, Dent.
Elegy for an Airman, Sydney, 1940, F. C. Johnson.
Sonnets to the Unknown Soldier, Sydney, 1941, Angus & Robertson.
* *The Fire on the Snow*, and *The Golden Lover*, Sydney, 1944, Angus & Robertson.
The Dosser in Springtime, Poems, Sydney, 1946, Angus & Robertson.
* *Ned Kelly*, Sydney, 1946, The Shepherd Press.
* *Shipwreck*, Sydney, 1947, The Shepherd Press.
Glencoe, Sydney, 1947, Angus & Robertson.
Sun Orchids and Other Poems, Sydney, 1952, Angus & Robertson.
VOGT, Anton:
Anti All That, Christchurch, 1940, Caxton.
Poems for a War, Wellington, 1943, Progressive.
Love Poems, Christchurch, 1952, Caxton.
WILSON, Patrick Seymour:
The Bright Sea, Christchurch, N.D. (1951), Pegasus.
WITHEFORD, Hubert:
Shadow of the Flame, Poems 1942–7, Auckland, 1950, Pelorus.
The Falcon Mask, Christchurch, N.D. (1951), Pegasus.
WRIGHT, David McKee:
Aorangi and Other Verses, Dunedin, 1896, Mills Dick.
Station Ballads and Other Verses, Dunedin, 1897, J. G. Sawell.

319

WRIGHT—*cont.*

New Zealand Chimes, Wellington, 1900, W. J. Lankshear.

Wisps of Tussock, Omaru, 1900, A. Fraser.

An Irish Heart, Sydney, 1918, Angus & Robertson.

JOINT PRODUCTIONS

Curnow, Fairburn, Glover: *Another Argo*, Christchurch, 1935, Caxton.

Curnow, Fairburn, Glover, Mason: *Recent Poems*, Christchurch, 1941, Caxton.

Baxter, Johnson, Vogt: *Poems Unpleasant*, Christchurch, 1952, Pegasus.

CAXTON COLLECTIONS

New Poems, 1934, includes Brasch, Curnow, Fairburn, Glover, Mason.

Verse Alive, 1936, includes Beaglehole, Curnow, Fairburn, Glover.

A Caxton Miscellany of Poems, *Verse*, *&c.*, 1937, includes Curnow, Fairburn, Glover, Hyde.

Verse Alive, *Number Two*, 1937, includes Beaglehole, Curnow, Dowling, Fairburn, Glover, Hyde, Mason.

ANTHOLOGIES
(*a selected list*)

Literary Foundlings, [no editor stated], Christchurch, 1864, 'at *The Times* Office'.

The Book of Canterbury Rhymes, [no editor stated], Christchurch, 1866, Ward & Reeves. Second edition, edit. W. P. Reeves, Christchurch, 1883, *Lyttelton Times* Publishing Co.

Australian Ballads and Rhymes, edit. D. B. W. Sladen, London, 1888, W. Scott.

Australian Poets, *1788–1888*, edit. D. B. W. Sladen, London, 1888, W. Scott.

The Jubilee Book of Canterbury Rhymes, edit. O. T. J. Alpers, Christchurch, 1900, Whitcombe & Tombs.

New Zealand Verse, edit. W. F. Alexander and A. E. Currie, London, 1906, W. Scott. Revised and enlarged edn., Auckland, 1926, Whitcombe & Tombs.

The Old Clay Patch, many eds., Wellington, 1910, Whitcombe & Tombs. Second edition, 1920: Third revised edition, 1949, N.Z. University Press.

The Oxford Book of Australasian Verse, edit. W. Murdoch, London, 1918, Oxford University Press. Revised as *A Book of Australasian Verse*, edit. W. Murdoch, London, 1924, Oxford University Press, and reprinted in 1928 and 1936. Revised as *A Book of Australasian Verse*, edit. W. Murdoch, Melbourne, 1945, Oxford University Press. Revised and enlarged as *A Book of Australian and New Zealand Verse*, edit. W. Murdoch and A. Mulgan, Melbourne, 1950, Oxford University Press.

An Australasian Anthology, edit. P. Serle, Sydney and Auckland, 1927, Collins. Second edition, 1929; third enlarged edition, 1946.

Kowhai Gold, edit. Q. Pope, London and Toronto, 1930, Dent.

Lyric Poems of New Zealand, 1928–1942, edit. C. A. Marris, Wellington, N.D. (1942), H. H. Tombs.

A Book of New Zealand Verse, 1923–45, edit. A. Curnow, Christchurch, 1945, Caxton. Second enlarged (1923–50) edition, 1951.

A Centennial Treasury of Otago Verse, edit. A. E. Currie, Christchurch, 1949, Caxton.

New Zealand Farm and Station Verse, 1850–1950, edit. A. E. Woodhouse, Christchurch, 1950, Whitcombe & Tombs.

Jindyworobak Anthology, 1951, edit. G. Rawlinson and W. Hart-Smith, Melbourne, 1952, Jindyworobak.

New Zealand Best Poems, 1932 to 1943, Wellington, H. H.
Tombs. Edited by C. A. Marris.

Arts Year Book, 1945 to 1951, Wellington, H. H. Tombs.
Poetry section edited by A. R. D. Fairburn.

Verse, 1950 and 1951, Wellington, the Glenco. No editor
stated.

New Zealand Poetry Yearbook, 1951 to 1953, Wellington, A. H.
& A. W. Reed; from 1954, Christchurch, Pegasus.
Edited by Louis Johnson.

PERIODICALS

Arachne. Irregular. Three numbers from January 1950 to
December 1951, the first published by the Victoria
University College Literary Society, Wellington, the last
two by the Crocus Publishing Co., Ltd., Wellington.
Various editors.

Arena. Approximately quarterly, beginning with no. 11,
March 1946, when it succeeded to ten numbers of
Letters. Published by the Handcraft Press, Wellington,
and edited by N. F. Hoggard.

Art in New Zealand. A quarterly, from September 1928 to
June 1944; the literary section of nos. 1 to 58 being
edited by C. A. Marris. Succeeded to by *The Arts in New
Zealand*, five issues from January to October 1945. Published by Harry H. Tombs Ltd., and directed throughout by H. H. Tombs.

Book. Irregular. Nine numbers from March 1941 to July
1947. Published by the Caxton Press, Christchurch.
No editor stated.

Gaudeamus. Approximately monthly from April to October 1951. Published and edited by Michael Conway, Anne Osborn and James Erikson, students at Canterbury University College, Christchurch.

Hilltop. Irregular. Three numbers from April to September 1949. Published by the Victoria University College Literary Society, Wellington. Various editors.

Landfall. A quarterly beginning in March 1947. Published by the Caxton Press, Christchurch, and edited by Charles Brasch.

New Zealand Listener. A weekly published for the New Zealand Broadcasting Service at Wellington. Edited until 1949 by Oliver Duff and since by M. H. Holcroft.

New Zealand New Writing. Irregular. Four numbers, the first two undated [1943?], the last two in June 1944 and March 1945. Published by the Progressive Publishing Society and edited by Ian A. Gordon.

Numbers. Irregular. Begun in July 1954. Editors and publishers not stated.

Phoenix. Irregular. Four numbers from March 1932 to June 1933. Published by the Auckland University College Students' Association and edited first by James Bertram and then by R. A. K. Mason.

Poetry, a Quarterly of Australian and New Zealand Verse. First nine issues undated, but from approximately December 1941 to July 1948. Published and edited by Flexmore Hudson, Lucindale, South Australia.

The Bulletin. A weekly published by the Bulletin Newspaper Co. Pty. Ltd., Sydney. The literary section ('the Red Page') at present edited by Douglas Stewart.

The Lyttelton Times. A daily newspaper which first published many poems by the Canterbury colonists.

The Outlook. A weekly, published and edited for the Presbyterian Church of New Zealand by A. M. Richards at Christchurch.

The Wooden Horse. Irregular. Eight numbers dated from April 1950 to 1951. Published and edited for the Bruce-Tuapeka Publishing Co. by C. R. Allen, first at Lawrence and then at Dunedin.

The publications of the students' associations of the colleges —particularly their annuals—occasionally contain poetry of worth, usually by graduates. We have included poems which first appeared in *Ako-Pai* (Wellington Teachers' Training College), *Canta* and *Canterbury University College Review* (Canterbury University College, Christchurch), *Kiwi* (Auckland University College), and *Spike* (Victoria University College, Wellington).

INDEX OF AUTHORS

INDEX OF TITLES AND FIRST LINES

Titles in *italic* type; first lines in roman

334

335

337